H.O.L.D.
F.A.S.T

Ride out LIFE
with Bipolar Disorder

Your Lifeboat in 8 Steps

A. GRIEME

Copyright © 2022 **A Grieme Books**

All rights reserved. No part of this publication may be reproduced, distributed, or transmitted in any form or by any means, including photocopying, recording, or other electronic or mechanical methods, without the prior written permission of the publisher, except in the case of brief quotations embodied in critical reviews and certain other noncommercial uses permitted by copyright law. For permission requests, write to the publisher, addressed "Attention: Book Rights and Permission," at the address below.

Published in the United States of America

ISBN 978-1-958518-78-6 (SC)
ISBN 978-1-958518-79-3 (HC)
ISBN 978-1-958518-77-9 (Ebook)

A Grieme Books
222 West 6th Street
Suite 400, San Pedro, CA, 90731
www.stellarliterary.com

Ordering Information and Rights Permission:

Quantity sales. Special discounts might be available on quantity purchases by corporations, associations, and others. For details, contact the publisher at the address above.

For Book Rights Adaptation and other Rights Permission. Call us at tollfree 18889458513 or send us an email at admin@stellarliteray.com.

This book is dedicated to my bipolar shipmates and to everyone who believes in us despite our fleeting whims and inconsistencies. Thank you. It means everything.

CONTENTS

CHAPTER 1:
YOU CAN MANAGE BIPOLAR DISORDER AND HAVE A GREAT LIFE 1

CHAPTER 2:
HOW I MANEUVERED MY UNSTABLE SLOOP FOR MOTHERHOOD 11

CHAPTER 3:
THE HOLD FAST METHOD IS *YOUR* LIFEBOAT 25

CHAPTER 4:
***H* IS FOR *HONEST*—TRANSPARENCY IS THE KEY TO COPE**. 32

CHAPTER 5:
***O* IS FOR *OPEN A DIALOGUE*—EXPLORE YOUR ILLNESS** 41

CHAPTER 6:
***L* IS FOR *LOOK TO YOUR HEART,* NOT YOUR CLUTTERED MIND** 49

CHAPTER 7:
***D* IS FOR *DISCERN TRIGGERS WITH LOGIC* FOR CLARITY** 57

CHAPTER 8:
***F* IS FOR *FACE ANXIETY* AND DIVE IN** 65

CHAPTER 9:
***A* IS FOR *ANTICIPATE FEAR*—EXPECT, EMBRACE, AND EXPERIENCE IT** 71

CHAPTER 10:
***S* IS FOR *STEP UP* TO YOUR FAMILY CHALLENGES** 79

CHAPTER 11:
T IS FOR *TRUST THE PROCESS*—TRUST YOURSELF 90
CHAPTER 12:
WHAT IF THE WHATIFS NEVER HAPPEN? 99
CHAPTER 13:
HOLD FAST—IT IS YOUR BEGINNING 110
ABOUT THE AUTHOR 116
THANK YOU 118

CHAPTER 1

YOU CAN MANAGE BIPOLAR DISORDER AND HAVE A GREAT LIFE

May what I do flow from me like a river, no forcing and no holding back, the way it is with children.

—Rainer Maria Rilke

The struggle of bipolar disorder is real. It is not tangible to many, which makes it difficult to understand. It is not uncommon that people who live and love with bipolar disorder, or any mental illness for that matter, are oftentimes misunderstood. Bipolar disorder knows no boundaries and does not discriminate. Many times, it is an insidious diagnosis that refuses to be ignored, requiring a host of psychiatric medications to assist in stabilizing the patient. In my humble experience, the medication is sometimes more debilitating than the illness itself; the host of side effects that it causes will leave a patient with a chemical imbalance or a mental affliction incapacitated and unable to function, work, and/or parent.

That is why the World Health Organization deemed bipolar disorder the sixth leading cause of disability in the world in 2019 (https://www.dbsalliance.org/). It is generally not visible from the outside but tears apart the sufferer and causes major emotional, psychological, and physical challenges in her life and the lives of those around her.

Despite the grim forecast, there is a silver lining. There is a way to manage bipolar disorder so that you can live, work at something you love, and spend valuable moments with your children and family. You can live with bipolar disorder, learn to find contentment in the discontent, and chuckle at the lunacy of it all. You can manage your bipolar disorder so that you will not fail your family or yourself. You can and you will stay afloat in this evercycling existence. There is a lifeboat.

Through a quarter of a century of experience with trial and error and pure passion, I am living proof that there is a way to maneuver and manage bipolar disorder to create a more harmonious atmosphere. You will rekindle your confidence in parenthood, despite your mental affliction and history. There is hope and it is figuratively tattooed across your knuckles, like a sailor who would hold fast to the lines when their ship was aloft in bad weather so he wouldn't be thrown off into the salty abyss— *HOLD FAST.*

HOLD FAST, tattooed across the knuckles of sailors, traditionally symbolized survival from a shipwreck, and superstitious sailors also believed that it was a symbol of protection from drowning. The *HOLD FAST* method is literally and figuratively the same thing, only a methodology that will keep you afloat in the oftentimes emotionally stormy existence of bipolar disorder. The HOLD FAST method will provide you with eight steps to ride out the changeable, sometimes turbulent sea of emotion inherent with bipolar disorder. You will be the best person that you can be, despite your whims and inconsistencies.

Case One:

I had an epiphany last year, all thanks to a beautiful woman that I will endearingly refer to as Mrs. D. While teaching eighthgrade humanities at a private school in Pennsylvania, Mrs. D came in to talk to me about her daughter's progress during a regularly scheduled conference. Her daughter, the eldest of two, was about to embark on a journey into young adulthood; she was applying to boarding schools to further her education, much to her mother's chagrin. Mrs. D was excited about her daughter's passion to go to a boarding school, but couldn't help but think that her daughter had chosen this route to get away from home.

When I asked, carefully, why she would think that would be a possibility, she started to cry and apologized for her tears. I carefully closed my door and opened my ear to her.

"Mrs. D, I am a mom too. I get it. If you need to talk, please let me be your ear. Your daughter is a wonderful girl and will flourish wherever she chooses to grace next year," I reassured her.

Mrs. D lifted her soulful brown eyes and reached for my hands across the table. "I read your story, Ms. Grieme. I know what you have been through, and I want you to know how much I admire your courage."

I was embarrassed that she had read my novel *Paging Dr. Freedman,* as mental illness still seems stigmatized in the world of education. But I laughed and shook off the compliment. "Oh, that's sweet, Mrs. D, but that novel is simply *based* on my experience with mental illness... It is predominantly fictitious."

> Mrs. D looked me straight in the eye. "You can't kid a kidder, Ms. G. I have struggled with bipolar disorder my entire adult life. I don't know how you do it. I have been a nurse, an educator, a retail clerk, barista... I can't hold a job. My children are my job, and I can't seem to do that right, either." She wept. "I don't think they know who I am from one day to the next, you see? That is why my little girl

wants to go away to boarding school. She wants *away from me!"*

All the consoling in the world would not have helped Mrs. D in that moment, although I tried. She was convinced that she was the worst parent in the history of the world and that she had no purpose. Thanks to her, that was the day I knew *my purpose*. My role as a mental health awareness advocate and educator had to step it up and take on peers who struggle. No more pretending. I had to be transparent; I somehow got through, and I needed to help my sisters and brothers who needed me.

I took on my first client outside of teaching students, and through helping Mrs. D, I developed the *HOLD FAST* method, inspired by knuckle tattoos on my husband's hands, weathered from years of motorcycling, tree work, and challenges of his own with mental afflictions.

Through our conversations, I learned so much about Mrs. D that I would have never been privy to had we not developed a friendship. She was thirty-nine and a mother of two beautiful young girls, nine and fourteen, and a wonderful *actor*—the great pretender, like myself. She struggles with rapid cycling bipolar disorder, a paradoxical and dizzying existence. I know from my own experience. Her life, up to that point, had been very tumultuous. Yet despite the self abuse inherent with imbalance, she was somehow able to maintain a sense of "normalcy" in her everyday facade in public and for her children.

She had been diagnosed at the age of eighteen with rapid cycling bipolar disorder with intermittent schizophrenic delusions; she selfmedicated for the most part. It was not until she became pregnant for her first daughter when she was twentyfiveyearsold that she understood the weight of her illness. She finally embraced that she needed to take it more seriously before she lost her life accidentally—or deliberately.

She moved home with her parents and staved off drugs and alcohol during her pregnancy. After her daughter was born, she eventually married the father, who had a steady occupation as an over-the-road truck driver.

Although her partner is very kind and patient, he was, and still is, only home on weekends, adding to her frustration. There is a palpable tension between them that is ever present because of her resentment toward his absence and her annoyance when he is present physically but not emotionally. The addition of crying children, menial tasks, and unjustifiable loneliness send her into a spiral of selfdoubt that literally *sink* her.

Mrs. D feels forced to cry in closets and around corners, as she refuses to allow her children to see her suffer. She thinks she is protecting her daughters, and although they may not see her struggle, they inevitably feel it; she teeters on the edge of an edge that she knows she cannot fall into again, or her children will suffer either with or without her. She needs tools to cope and someone outside of her circle to confide in. She needs the security of knowing that she can climb out of a dark place when her children need her. She needs to know that she is not alone; she *can* and *will* overcome this.

Characteristic of many I have known with this illness, including myself, on a superficial level, professionally and in the eyes of the public, Mrs. D is jovial with limitless creativity and painfully optimistic. At the core of her being, that is who she is, yet her main struggle is with motherhood and balancing home life. Her constant needling fear is that her instability will rear its ugly head and negatively impact her family. The majority of her energy blankets her children to create a sense of stability for them, leaving her running on a dwindling reserve for everything else.

Although she moves forward out of necessity, she can't help but flounder; it is the human condition. And in her case, despite the fact that she has left selfmedication and vices behind her, the everpresent confusion, fog, and struggles of bipolar disorder are still there. At times, she finds herself emotionally and physically incapacitated; finding any balance becomes seemingly impossible. The everevolving demands of motherhood and family have become progressively more difficult for her to cope with. Instead of reaching out for assistance, she internalizes everything. She avoids friends and family and saves what little energy she has to give to her children.

Now, 14 years later, as a mother of two and wife

despite many odds, Mrs. D takes her illness very seriously. But despite consistently taking her prescribed medication to help her stabilize, I learned that she still struggles with self medication and addiction in secret. It is behind closed doors where she unravels. When this happens, her parents begrudgingly jump in, and her husband extends his overtheroad trucking trips to avoid the chaos. Mrs. D resents *his* inability to father but depends on his income to survive. Her daughters have each other, but inevitably feel the weight of their mother's pain.

While working with Mrs. D and listening to her struggle, my empathy allowed me to dive deeply into my own experience with bipolar disorder, where I created eight steps that I used to keep me afloat during this oftentimes turbulent sea of existence, inspired by sailors holding on to the mast for dear life in a storm, and my husband's weathered tattooed hands, which have endured many storms of their own.

The Eight Steps I Created and

Utilize That Have Helped Her Through:

- *H* is for *honest*
- *O* is for *open a dialogue*
- *L* is for *look to your heart*
- *D* is for *discern with logic*
- *F* is for *face anxiety*
- *A* is for *anticipate fear*

H.O.L.D. F.A.S.T.

- *S* is for *step up*
- *T* is for *trust the process*

Each of these steps has been, and continue to be, my lifeboat. I shared how I implemented each of these steps into my struggle with mental illness to overcome and *just be* with Mrs. D; I wanted her to truly understand that she is steering her own ship. She is in control, and *not* her disease.

After working together, Mrs. D, my inspiration and catalyst for change, has implemented *my HOLD FAST* method into her life. She has since left her closet vices behind and has made simple lifestyle choices that have created drastic changes in her world. She has reentered the world of education as a high school English teacher at a charter arts school and walks to school every day with her eldest daughter, now a sophomore visual arts student. I can proudly say that she now surfs the wave of parenthood and family as the best mother she can be and shares her story with those who falter. She is *truly* an inspiration, and I know she will share her learned methodology with someone who needs it.

In summary, bipolar disorder, among many other mental diseases, is great at hiding in our shadows, behind smiles and painfully exhausting facades of "normalcy" (whatever that is supposed to look like). In life, the stigma that is still inherent among the mentally ill forces the mentally ill to remain quiet about their harrowing experience, for fear of not being taken seriously, ridiculed, or judged. Unlike a broken bone or a bleeding laceration, mental illness is still treated differently by the medical world; there are no casts, stitches, or bandages for a chemical imbalance. But there are ways to think differently that can improve your way of life. In chapter 2, I share my personal experience with bipolar disorder, how each step of the *HOLD FAST* method manifested itself in my life, and how I overcame my own mental illness to focus on motherhood. I found my lifeboat.

CHAPTER 2

HOW I MANEUVERED MY UNSTABLE SLOOP FOR MOTHERHOOD

> Please could you stop the noise I'm trying to get some rest…from all the unborn chicken voices in my head.
>
> —Radiohead

In hindsight, I feel like my late teens and early 20s were a necessary unraveling to unearth this new understanding. That person was shrouded in insecurity, the antithesis of *HOLD FAST*.

- *H* is for *honest*
- *O* is for *open a dialogue*
- *L* is for *look to your heart*
- *D* is for *discern with logic*

- *F* is for *face anxiety*
- *A* is for *anticipate fear*
- *S* is for *step up*
- *T* is for *trust the process*

The Truth

- I was seldom honest with anyone about anything, especially myself.
- I was aware that I was suffering, but instead of opening any dialogue, I shut down and masked any truth with drugs and alcohol.
- I hadn't any idea how to deal with the pain. My heart was perpetually broken.
- I could not decipher the logical from the illogical.
- I would smother any anxiety with substances; if they were not available, I would hide.
- I did not anticipate fear but dreaded impending fear, instead.
- I did not face anything ugly for fear of confrontation. Avoidance was my method of choice. Asking for help was a sign of weakness.
- I trusted those who should not have been trusted and refused to trust in things or people that would help me.

The list of things wrong was deep and dark as the ocean; I was drowning. I didn't know who the hell I was, nor did I care. I was simply a 20-year-old girl with what I thought was an artistic temperament, a penchant for drugs, alcohol, the male persuasion, and flights of fancy with a wicked streak when under the influence. I thought I knew everything. Others eventually convinced me otherwise; I toyed with the idea of help to pacify my family.

Alas, my selfabsorption index, inherent in the mentally ill, was at an alltime high when I was 20 and diagnosed with bipolar disorder. I thought it all a joke; I felt like a pawn of some kind. Having studied Freud and Jung in freshman psychology 101, I simply thought that the psychiatrist who diagnosed me was playing games with my mind.

I was convinced that I was far more superior to him and thought that it was all hyperbolic bullshit that he was feeding me. Psychiatric jargon (id, ego, superego) was all stuff fed to the minds of us evolving into adulthood. It was all part of some elaborate chess game that boxed me into whatever it was that I was supposed to become.

But I took the meds anyway because why not? They added a new affect. I partied, I drank, and I fell deeper into confusion, somehow maintaining a life as a successful student. I lived a paradoxical existence. And with every flight of fancy and manic moment, there was an equally dark underbelly waiting to surface. My mixed states were wild; I was blinded by excitement and debilitated by sadness in tandem.

That was my normal.

And then I took an advertising and propaganda class. I loved it! That particular day, I was the proud recipient of the highest mark on one of my essays that I wrote; the professor read it aloud. The essay was an extensive study entitled "Adverting's Portrayal of the Female Body and Its Effect on Women Plagued with Eating Disorders." I was inspired to write it because of my roommate's struggle with bulimia. Or maybe it was the fact that after seeing a series of very unflattering photographs of myself, a *boyfriend du jour* of mine commented on a headshot of a waiflike model in a magazine and said that I sort of reminded him of her..."A little." He carefully examined her image. "Your face, anyway." He shrugged, and I was well aware of what that meant. The seed was planted.

The campaign I focused on was the early 1990s Calvin Klein Campaign. I was fascinated by the androgyny of the models; I found the David Bowieesque appeal painfully attractive but was revolted by the thought that perhaps the images lent themselves as detrimental to anorexic and bulimic young women. Or so I thought. That was my women's studies angle, I guess. The truth was shrouded in selfloathing and came to fruition for me that evening.

The advertisement I chose for my study was iconic. It was at the height of the *Calvin Klein Obsession* Campaign featuring the very young waiflike, almost

H.O.L.D. F.A.S.T.

prepubescent-looking Kate Moss. She was featured nude and strategically positioned in photographs to spell sex with her angular elbows and knees. Her pallor was that of a junkie who just emerged from a Turkish bath, sans makeup and heavylidded.

Her cheekbones were wideset, perfect hollows in her sallow cheeks. To me, she was the perfect cross between a Native American goddess and a jilted medieval serf, like a Celtic faery morphed with Sacagawea. Her mouth was slightly agape, showing a hint of Bardot (esque) gapped teeth... her chestnut hair was haphazardly swept off her face. Her eyes peered into my soul, whispering, *"I am who you are. I am who you will be. I am beautiful, and you can be, too."*

She was, indeed, who I *wanted* to be, not representative of something I was deeply appalled by. She was perfection, photographed in black and white. I saw myself in her, and I became compulsively preoccupied. I was smitten with her image, the image that I was supposed to mirror if I were to be considered attractive, too. That image would make me whole, take away my sadness, erratic mood swings, jealousy, anger, envy, violent happiness—everything that I felt when I was in a mixed state, unknowingly. Her image was the honesty I sought; being *her* would make me whole again.

That particular evening, after a night of drinking and celebrating my successful women's studies endeavor, I took the long walk from the drinking hovels on the main street of my college town toward home before last call. I caught my drunken reflection in a store window under a streetlight. That is where I saw myself— a stumbling contradiction, a miserable hypocrite. I saw a girl who didn't hold a candle to the image in her mind, and even less of a candle to her beautiful, eating disorder—riddled roommate. I saw a girl who was flawed, thick, drunk, dumpy, shuffling along in faux fur and dirty Vans. I saw the girl that everyone else saw, and she wasn't good enough. She was vain but ugly. A failure. A mess. A waste of life. A joke.

I fidgeted with the cigarettes in my pocket, fumbling for a lighter, walked closer to my reflection, and watched ghosts of smoke rise up toward the streetlamp into the night. I walked closer and closer to my image, noticing every flaw. Every unkind word that had ever been said to me about my physical appearance, every false friend that had betrayed me was justified. I really wasn't worth it.

I stared at my disheveled body under the 2:00 AM lamplight into my own green eyes, despite snickers from passersby. I realized with every exhale of my cigarette, I was a disgrace. It was true. I wasn't a good friend or a well-informed young woman advocating for the health and wellbeing of my cohorts. I was a phony. I was nothing. I was not Kate Moss sprawled like an angelic junkie waif on the back cover of *Elle.* In fact, I couldn't find her in my drug-addled, beer drowned reflection; that is the truth as to why I was so, so sad.

H.O.L.D. F.A.S.T.

I shuffled over the bridge toward my home in the dark, wondering if I could just disappear completely right there, into the icy water below. It seemed the perfect opportunity. I was alone. It was almost the weekend. No one would question my disappearance for at least a day or two, and even that was debatable. By then, I would've floated to the Atlantic and become bloated, unrecognizable fish food—end of story. No more boxing matches in my young brain. No more hypocrisy. No more heartache. I chuckled at the sky, amused by the irony once again. Hours earlier, I was elated, proud, a strong young woman making a difference with her innovative thinking and writing. I was out of control; I felt it.

I climbed onto the railing and sat smoking, teetering on the edge of the bridge, watching the night sky warble in the water below, when a truck pulled over. It was a girl I hardly knew from one of my classes.

"Need a ride?"

I fumbled with another smoke, unable to light it with a match. She pulled over, put the truck in park, and walked carefully over to me with a lighter. Her boyfriend sat watching from the passenger's seat. She cupped our hands and lit my smoke.

"Thanks." I inhaled.

"Yeah!" She smiled. She surveyed my seat on the railing of the bridge.

"Come down from there. It's cold. Hop in! I'll take you home." She was wearing a mini skirt, and her skinny little legs were shivering in the streetlight.

And that was it. That was the moment that I knew something was terribly wrong, I was aware that when I jumped into her truck, I felt fine, completely fine, like better than I'd felt all day. I rattled on and on about how beautiful the river looks at night, and how I love the night air, and how lucky we are to have the freedom to appreciate night. She smiled agreeably at me and drove toward my infamous house, a den of iniquity for many. When we arrived, I thanked them both profusely for the lift.

"Oh wow...so rude of me. You guys want to come in and have a couple beers? Smoke a joint? I'm sure someone else is still up, too." I smiled.

I saw her boyfriend, who hadn't spoken a word roll his eyes, then followed his hand down to her shivering knee; he gave a gentle squeeze. Her knees were perfectly bony, like Kate Moss. I silently compared mine to hers.

"Ah, it's late. Class in the morning." She shrugged. "Get some sleep." She waved and pulled away in her little Toyota pickup.

Deep, deep sadness settled back in as I wandered into the house, past my room, through the silent living space, and into the bathroom. I traced a tear down my face in the mirror and watched it disappear into my mouth. I wanted to shed my skin. I wanted to peel off my layers like an onion. I wanted the sadness gone.

I gagged myself until I threw up everything that I could. And with every gag, I felt like a piece of me was connecting, like a puzzle. My shattered image of myself pieced together like broken glass. My old me was gone; I would become Calvin Klein's waif, at any cost. It was a new beginning for me. My image in the mirror would dictate my mood for years to come.

Two weeks later at my next psychiatrist appointment, I proudly strutted into the waiting room in a wool miniskirt, thighhigh tights, and a wooly sweater. I was on top of the world, ten pounds lighter, and closer to my goal. I had taken on a catwalk of sorts, and it felt good.

"Wow! You look happier, Amanda.

The medication seems to be helping you, yes?"

"Yes, Doc, I feel good. I'm walking everywhere, I'm eating well, I'm sleeping, not drinking... as much." I gave him a sideways smile. He seemed to believe my lies, and that made me feel powerful. I hadn't actually taken my meds in days.

He winked. "You look thinner." He smiled. "It really becomes you."

He patted me on the knee, and I giggled like a schoolgirl. *Thinner* was what I wanted to hear; I was elated! So even thinner I would become; that is what the male persuasion thinks becomes me, so it must be the truth. My truth. That was something I could control. That would make me happy again.

That warped thinking overcame me like smog well into my 30s. Even when I felt a sense of stability, the girl in the 2:00 AM lamplight would rear her ugly head, holding me below the surface, gasping and reaching for something to help me stay afloat:

- *H* is for *honest*
- *O* is for *open a dialogue*
- *L* is for *look to your heart*
- *D* is for *discern with logic*
- *F* is for *face anxiety*
- *A* is for *anticipate fear*
- *S* is for *step up*
- *T* is for *trust the process*

And then the universe gave me the ultimate gift; my purpose became crystal clear. All the steps became my reality with the birth of my daughter, River. She happened when I was 37-years-old and is why I *HOLD FAST*.

Now, many moons later, I live to share how I stay afloat in this ever-cycling existence as her mother. Dizzying as life may feel sometimes, my daughter has officially saved *me* from *myself*; children are remarkable that way. Motherhood was the catalyst for a metamorphosis. It was just the beginning of a necessary

H.O.L.D. F.A.S.T.

transcendence, the first step in separating from the ensnaring diagnosis of rapid cycling bipolar disorder that would not allow itself to be ignored, despite the copious amounts of blue and pink imagination slayers that I was prescribed and took, for the most part.

I was forced to be honest with myself with the onset of motherhood. I grieved, and I held tight to the want-to-be existential ways of *myself*. The breakup was intense! But that moment when I realized the responsibility of another life was in my arms, *myself* resentfully climbed out of my mind and leaped one arm's length away from *me*. That was the moment that motherhood made *me* get over *myself*.

Before motherhood, I could never understand (or cared to, for that matter) things like security and financial planning, career goals—too boring. I had no capacity to think ahead: there was just *now*. Not out of lack of motivation or laziness but due to an inability to focus on something less than interesting (perhaps necessary) to me for more than a few seconds. Anything beyond short term wasn't important; it would all work out or it just wouldn't be. Everything was as it should've been, regardless.

I loved the urgency of now, laughter in the moment, the party—the pendulum.

I didn't listen to anyone who questioned my whims and inconsistencies. I never dreamed of a magical wedding, a white gown, or a prince charming. It all seemed preposterous. I did what felt right. That is how I lived. That is who I was. I wanted to see what would happen next, but not too many steps beyond that.

I loved to *live*, board a plane, and go somewhere new; strangers were new friends who never had to become old friends. My passions were deep as oceans; I felt everything, and then I felt nothing in a single breath. I was simply coexisting with existence. Now I *know*. I am a mama, and I understand thinking ahead. It's a forced issue. My self-absorption index has dwindled into nothingness. Mentally and emotionally, I accepted this new role kicking and screaming but have never felt more, well...stable, alive, honest.

I didn't succumb to the illness; that was my choice. I live with it like a roommate. She is difficult yet loveable, sometimes home too long, sometimes gone for days. Often, she is punctual with the rent, many times she shirks *all* responsibility. Sometimes, she is deliciously fun and inspiring, though often infinitely dark. She, *myself*, is always there at arm's length.

Myself is an appendage of my totality; she can overcome like a thick fog but will dutifully go back to her room, back to her chrysalis state, when my daughter needs *me*. It is my choice. Although she still suffocates me sometimes or fills me with violent happiness that blinds my senses, she ultimately enjoys solitude. The sound of a child needing something, anything, sends her

H.O.L.D. F.A.S.T.

back to the cocoon in a huff. She just cannot be bothered with such *trivialities*.

Me (on the other hand) has both hands on the ship lines in the storm, both goofy-footed feet on the surfboard in the waves. *Myself* simply hangs below deck or curls up on a lonely spot on the beach, slugging rum and feeling sorry for herself, whereas me has chosen to *HOLD FAST*. "This, too, shall pass," she says. *Me* found her lifeboat.

In closing, I leave you with some of my favorite words from the *30 Day Mental Diet* by Willis Kinnear. His words and lessons have resonated with me since I happened upon them many moons ago. When it is imperative that we, as parents, have to move forward, regardless of our mental state for the sake of parenting, please remember this: "Strange as it sounds, it is impossible for you to fail. For if you fail you have succeeded in being a failure!"

Kinnear continues, "For the most part people feel that they are a success in an endeavor when it has a favorable outcome, and a failure when it is not accomplished." But this is not necessarily true. Closer consideration will show that success is the achievement of the dominant idea you have in mind, and what you achieve always corresponds to your thinking. In this respect you never fail, you always succeed.

Favorable or not does not enter into the matter.

In summary, everyone has a backstory; mental illness does not discriminate, and manifests itself differently at different stages of your life. The stories are seldom pleasant, and many times scarring and disturbing to those who experience them. The key to moving beyond the backstory—the 2:00 AM lamplight image in a dark window that haunts you—is to let go and float to the surface, swim forward, and focus on the positive. Climb into the lifeboat; that is where you will find yourself.

Your backstory is just that, a backstory. It is one of the many facets that make up the beautiful being that is you. It is just a tiny piece, one that adds character to the overall amazing puzzle called you. You are not your mental illness; it does not define you. Be honest with yourself. You, too, can stay afloat, manage your bipolar disorder, and be the best person you can be. Chapter 3 explores the importance of your lifeboat and how it will make it easier for you to open your door to clarity and communication. Climb into your lifeboat that keeps you afloat; we all have one. In our boats, if we choose to utilize them, there are many important tools to help you move forward.

CHAPTER 3

THE HOLD FAST METHOD IS *YOUR* LIFEBOAT

Since everything is a reflection of our minds...
everything can be changed by our minds.

—Gautama Buddha

Think of your lifeboat as your safe space without judgment. Your lifeboat is filled with invaluable, honest tools to keep you afloat as a person, above the stormy water and downward spiral. Your lifeboat has a few very important compartments that keep you level in the stormy waters of bipolar disorder when utilized. *HOLD FAST* to it:

- *H* is for *honest*

- *O* is for *open a dialogue*
- *L* is for *look to your heart*
- *D* is for *discern with logic*
- *F* is for *face anxiety*
- *A* is for *anticipate fear*
- *S* is for *step up*
- *T* is for *trust the process*

Lifeboat compartment #1 holds the honesty buoy. By inflating your honesty buoy to show your family and friends what is truly going on inside of your mind, you are opening a line of trust that may not have been there prior. Children, specifically, feel everything and are well aware that there is something amiss with you, despite you not having directly shared it. The best gift you can give them is the truth; they deserve to know so that they can process your sometimes erratic behavior differently and not feel as if it is somehow their fault. That only perpetuates confusion, continuing the cycle of unjustifiable mistrust. Simple communication is a lifesaver.

In lifeboat compartment #2, keep logic handy, as logic will help you rise to the surface when inundated with selfdoubt. It's ironic, actually. Everyone I have ever encountered with a form of bipolar disorder tend to seem highly illogical to some. But to themselves, their decisions make perfect sense. And that is perfectly fine. It is in delusional moments when the logic buoy comes in handy, as sometimes the decision making of the person in crisis

H.O.L.D. F.A.S.T.

needs a dose of external logic to modify his thinking.

Don't ignore the delusion or write it off as just a fleeting belief, but don't give it precedence in your mind, or it will become invasive. *Voice it. Then voice it again.* If you keep it inside, it can become potentially disastrous and overwhelm you. If you can take a deep breath, hang on to the logic lifesaver, and look your verbalized delusion in the eyes, you will be more likely to be able to calmly talk yourself out of the place that your thoughts are drowning. If it persists, there is great news; you are *aware* that something is off, and awareness is the key to understanding! Write it down. Share it with a confidante. Eventually, it will lose its power and fall away, sinking into the abyss of the bipolar sea.

There is a wonderful online resource that I recommend to my bipolar cohorts called *Challenge the Storm*. It is an idea with a mission, and a remarkable catharsis for those who need to share their story and connect with those who can commiserate. It offers invaluable advice because of its no BS approach and guileless portrayal of mental illness as it is: a state of disease that can be dealt with, given the right tools. Author and Penn State–trained mental health professional Zach Good notes,

Numerous mental disorders precipitate delusions, but the most common ones are schizophrenia, schizoaffective disorder, and bipolar mania. Typical delusions include persecutory delusions ('The government implanted a chip in my head to track me'), grandiose delusions ('I'm a famous rapper and I have a world tour kicking off next month), and delusions of reference ('When LeBron James pointed at the camera after making that gamewinning shot he was giving me a secret sign'). Good is a contributor for http://challengethestorm.org/.

Good illustrates a great example of the experience of a delusion due to bipolar disorder, schizophrenia or schizoaffective disorder, stating that a delusional person "might come to believe the mailman is a government spy based on the fact that the mailman goes to the individual's house every day. When forming that conclusion, they don't consider that the mailman also goes to every other house in the neighborhood every day, or that the mailman doesn't come by on Sundays and holidays, or that the mailman is a regular guy who lives across town and goes to high school football games on Friday nights. By asking the individual with the delusion how they account for these discrepancies, you force them to confront evidence they probably hadn't previously considered."

The same goes for you. When you breathe and get into the right space, selfquestioning is also effective because it gives you the opportunity to test your logic and put yourself in a different mindset, able to see another side of your story. Selfprobing for more information is valuable for several reasons: Ask yourself the following:

H.O.L.D. F.A.S.T.
1. Who?
2. What?
3. Where?
4. When?
5. Why?
6. How?

It is effective. You look at the thought(s) or the "story" in the third person, like a journalist, so you can make better sense of it. Most importantly, you are forced to articulate how you came to think whatever it is that is delusional. This thinking will oftentimes allow you to analyze the missing links in your own thought process. When you arrive at a delusion, you tend to make one giant leap from A to Z, missing several important steps along the way. When you jump out of your mind, holding the confusion, it is then that you can dissect it outside of yourself with logic and clarity. You can voice it, listen to it, then release it and let it fall away. It is then that you can float gently back into your heart space.

In lifeboat compartment #3, you will find the fear and anxiety anchors. Many times, you will do everything you can to avoid opening this compartment because it is so uncomfortable; you know how oppressive it can be. Alas, it is that very discomfort in fear and anxiety that allows you to float in peace on your lifeboat. You must experience the negative emotions, the unknown, embrace it like your own even as it scratches, bites, and tries to pull you under where you cannot breathe. You have to feel its weight, listen to it, speak to it, tell it how you feel, give it love, rock it gently, then allow it to silently fall to sleep in your arms. It is then and only then that you can let it go gently, watch it sink in hindsight, and float peacefully.

Something to note: The universe does not have favorites and your lifeboat does not judge you. Remember that.

Willis Kinnear, author of the *30Day Mental Diet,* explains a beautiful truth:

> Any law, in any sphere of activity, improperly used will bring improper results. In the physical world scientists are able to avail themselves of the power of nature only when they are able to ascertain the laws of its action and properly use them. You are in much the same position. You have to discover for yourself the nature of the spiritual Law which governs your experiences in living, and then properly apply it.

In other words, surf it. Don't try to swim against the current. Let life help you. Hold fast, sailor. Kinnear continues,

> When you properly understand this you will find that Life is for you; then you can avail yourself of all Its good in your life.

H.O.L.D. F.A.S.T.

You use the Law for your benefit. It is futile to battle against Its action; you direct Its action in the manner you desire. Your ability to direct this action resides in the nature of the Godgiven creative power of your own thought.

In summary, we all have a lifeboat with tools of survival available to us, if we just ask. We often become so lost in our own thoughts that we forget to share what is on our mind. We forget that we have options that will help us make sense of things. It is the letting go that lightens the load and allows us to float on in peace as the best version of ourselves. In chapter 4, you will understand that you must be honest and transparent about your condition and mental state as the first step in coping with it.

CHAPTER 4

H IS FOR *HONEST*—TRANSPARENCY IS THE KEY TO COPE

> Work of eyes is done. Go now and do the heart work on the images imprisoned within you.
>
> —Rainer Maria Rilke

Transparency is the key to understanding your illness. That is a universal truth and one that I couldn't comprehend fully until I was well advanced into my bipolar illness and much damage had already been done, physically, emotionally, and psychologically.

Since my initial diagnosis as a college sophomore, I spent the next ten or so years in the same loop, following the same cycle. Doctor's visits, lies about taking medication properly, drug abuse, identifying myself by what the male persuasion saw me as, on the verge of suicide in one breath and advising someone on how to save their own life in the next breath.

Until I crashed. And that time, I was helpless. Hospitalized, delusional, painfully thin, and living on cigarettes and red wine, my meds, and any other meds that didn't belong to me that I could get my hands on, I met my match, my honesty mirror. His name is Dr. Freedman, and he saved *me* from myself. He showed me the importance of telling the truth by calling me out on my bullshit. He didn't look at me as the object I thought I was but as an intellectual woman with heaps of potential and a chemical imbalance. He didn't tell me I was crazy or wrong for doing the things I had done to torture *myself.* Instead, he showed me that I am not alone. He treated mental illness as an osteopathic doctor would treat chronic back pain. Like an osteopathic doctor uses musculoskeletal manipulation, gentle pressure, and resistance to stretch the body to alleviate the symptoms and strengthen the core issue, Dr. Freedman did the same with my attitude toward healing from mental illness:

> You cannot cope with anything,
> Amanda, unless you understand it.

Dr. Freedman asked me to examine myself without judgment; he spoke to me as an equal. He told me that unless I start to look at my illness seriously, try medicine consistently, and learn about what rapid cycling bipolar is and not what I think it is, I was on a road to nowhere.

Because we both shared a passion for music, reading, and learning, he loaned me medical books, inspirational books (that didn't make me gag) about Eastern philosophy, and recommended beautiful classical and jazz selections for me to immerse myself in:

> Honesty will set you free and allow you
> to separate yourself from the illness.

He drove home how important it was for me to talk to people about how I feel. And when I told him that I loathe complaining, he laughed:

> And that's why you need to do it, Amanda. You hate it because you don't want to hear the truth outside of your own head. When you say it aloud, it is no longer stuck inside of you. You are not your bipolar disorder illness Amanda... just like I am not any of my maladies. You are simply a host, in charge of the symptoms. You have control over your actions and how you deal with your unwelcome guest.

It was that statement that separated me from my illness and all its manifestations. They were just guests—some welcome, some not. Some here, some gone. Some planning a visit, some never coming back, gratefully. I am in charge; I call the shots, and only I can get over myself and send self absorption packing with honesty, as will you!

I learned from Dr. Freedman that being honest was actually easier than being dishonest. Honesty doesn't require as much brainpower and is far less complicated than dishonesty. I found that if I told the truth, there was a period at the end of the sentence. If I fabricated some excuse, it only led to many more fabrications that required strings and strings of thoughts that eventually tangled together so tightly that I would strangle myself with disillusion. Honesty is just that—transparent. Right, wrong or indifferent, *it* just *is*.

Mental illness, in my world, was always the pink elephant in the living room. My family never spoke of my great grandmother who was left with two small children while her husband was off to sea as the captain of a ship called *The Queen Bermuda*. My grandfather Harry and his sister Hazel, neither of whom I ever met, were left without a mother at a very young age. While their father was out to sea, their mother sadly committed *suicide*. Whenever I brought it up, everyone changed the subject.

Finally, my paternal grandmother, Katarina, told me the rest of the story when I was a teenager. She said that it was never spoken of that Harry's mother suffered from depression. She was left for months at a time with two small children while her husband was out at sea. She was overwhelmed, to say the least. During one of her husband's brief visits home, she became pregnant, again.

She tried to self-abort, and hemorrhaged to death.

When my mother was born in 1945, her mother, my Nanny, had some serious postpartum issues, so I was told. In actuality, my mother was a very sick infant, premature, and raised for the first year of her life by a Norwegian au pair and her nineyearold sister, Natalie. When I finally asked, "So where was Nanny?" referring to her mother, Edna, it was explained, vaguely, that she wasn't well and was sent *away*. That was my maternal grandmother.

So when I turned about 13, I started to truly loathe life. I was quietly anguished, deeply insecure, and bullied by girls who said they were friends. Despite my inner turmoil, I exhibited a facade of perpetual happiness; I didn't understand that talking about it was an option. I had no idea that these emotions were acceptable and allowed to be voiced. And in my family, insecurity was a sign of weakness, and weakness was *not* okay. So I shut down.

My mother was, and still is, a vision of confidence: statuesque, beautiful, talented, warm, kind, loving, entrepreneurial, sassy, and smart. She *always* put on an air of *all is good*. That is all she knew. The truth was that she suffered in silence for years from debilitating anxiety and depression, but felt like if she voiced it, her world would fall apart. Like my mom, I never felt like I could share my reality with anyone.

I simply masked my illness with drugs and alcohol,

H.O.L.D. F.A.S.T.

starting at a very young age.

When I was well into my twenties, my mom had a complete meltdown and began to openly address her issues and voice them, without fear of stigma, with a lot of support from her very close friends, my dad, and a wonderful doctor. I watched in awe as my mother unraveled and mended herself, stitch by agonizing stitch, somehow keeping the family business afloat, and a sense of normalcy. Voicing it and getting the help she needed made all of the difference for her. I didn't know it then, but in hindsight, her courage for facing her mental issues was an inspiration for me. In fact, her transparency inadvertently kept me going many times when I truly didn't think that I had any purpose.

It was my mom and dad who I finally fell apart in front of for the first time and asked for help when I was about thirty; it hurt like hell to have to admit that I was not okay. Admitting there is a problem is the hardest part. They understood, asked no questions, and became my confidants and caretakers in a time when I was teetering on the edge. It was the first time I spoke transparently about my illnesses, and they listened. It was the beginning of a metamorphosis for me; honesty was the first step toward wellness.

Honesty is an integral part of selfimprovement and overcoming delusional thinking. If we aren't honest with ourselves, then we can't expect to learn and grow as individuals; without honesty, we aren't willing to recognize reality for what it is. When we are dishonest, we only choose to see what we want to see and ignore what we don't want to see. This may provide shortterm happiness or relief, but it is unhealthy and destructive over the course of time. Being honest with you can sometimes be painful, but it is the necessary component to longterm contentment.

Try these simple steps to achieve honesty:

1. You must acknowledge both the positive and negative. One common way you deceive yourself is by ignoring the negative aspects of your life. Sometimes it's easier to turn a blind eye to your problems rather than confront them. Be honest about both the good and bad. Create a mindset of acceptance. Seeing things as they really are makes them much more tangible.
2. Take time to write. Every evening before you fall asleep, ask yourself questions like, "How did things go today? What did I do right? What could I have done better?" Write down your thoughts, honestly, without judgment or criticism. You will inevitably sleep easier, having emptied your mind onto a blank piece of paper. It is very cathartic.
3. Own up to your mistakes. Many times you try to protect your ego by coming up with excuses or blaming others for your problems. When in

truth, only a person who admits her mistakes can learn from them and correct them. Ignoring mistakes will set the stage for repetition. Doing this in writing before sleeping is very therapeutic.
4. Pay attention to your feelings. While sometimes emotions can be misleading, they can also be very revealing. When you ask yourself the true cause behind your emotions, you will learn what thoughts, actions, and situations cause you to feel a certain way. That transparency will teach you how to respond to your emotions differently in the future.
5. Find someone you trust to be open with you. To be truly honest with yourself, you sometimes need an outside perspective. Friends and family, seemingly with good intentions, will often protect you from the things about yourself that you don't typically think about or pay attention to. In other words, they don't always call you out on your bullshit. That is why a completely outside perspective from someone who isn't a part of your daily life (therapist, counselor, or coach) provides you with honest answers.
6. Be a straight shooter. Being honest with yourself isn't about trying to intellectualize or rationalize everything that happens to you. Just be straightforward and matteroffact with

yourself. Note how things are in the moment and do your best.
7. Know your limitations. A necessary part of honesty is being aware of your limitations, including recognizing that you don't know everything. It keeps you humble, realistic, and open to new ideas. There is wisdom in ignorance if you're willing to acknowledge it and learn from it.

In summary, honesty is something you need to practice every day. It takes constant self awareness. When honesty meets your willingness to change, the results are remarkable. In chapter 5, you will understand that by opening yourself up and exploring your illness transparently, seeking support outside of your immediate circle will give you a different perspective on your situation. You *can* do this.

CHAPTER 5

O IS FOR *OPEN A DIALOGUE*—EXPLORE YOUR ILLNESS

And we'll all float on okay... And we'll all float on okay... And we'll all float on okay... And we'll all float on anyway, well.

—Modest Mouse

Of all the wonderful reading material that Dr. Freedman shared with me at my most vulnerable time in my life, the one that resonated most was *The Power of Now* by Eckhart Tolle. It was given to him at an obscured point in his career as an MD, and he read it despite his general distaste for anything that includes the words *spiritual* and *enlightenment*. I admire that about him.

When I contemplated sitting and talking with

someone for cognitive therapy, the idea gave me the chills. Even though my thoughts had become unhealthy, they were still my thoughts. Sharing them seemed like the ultimate insult to myself. When I happened upon this quote by Eckhart Tolle, it resonated with me, and resonates with me on a daily basis, years later as a mother, teacher, and mental health awareness advocate:

> A belief may be comforting. Only through your own experience, however, does it become liberating. Thinking has become a disease. Disease happens when things get out of balance. For example, there is nothing wrong with cells dividing and multiplying in the body, but when this process continues in disregard of the total organism, cells proliferate and we have disease. The mind is a superb instrument if used rightly. Used wrongly, however, it becomes very destructive. To put it more accurately, it is not so much that you use your mind wrongly—you usually don't use it at all. It uses you. This is the disease. You believe that you are your mind. This is the delusion. The instrument has taken you over.

In mental illness, I find that to liberate the feelings of doubt, delusion, negativity, sadness, irrational fear, et cetera, you have to liberate the thoughts because thoughts proliferate like cells. If you allow the thoughts to multiply upon themselves, they will create a web of confusion so dense and disconcerting that you cannot find your way out. Your mind, then, "uses" you, and you lose complete control of yourself, like I did. And in my time of selfinduced woe and confusion, the ones who suffered were the ones I love the most: my family:

> And that's why you need to do it, Amanda. You hate it because you don't want to hear the truth outside of your own head. When you say it aloud, it is no longer stuck inside of you.

Dr. Freedman's words rattled around in my brain. I had to speak. Opening a dialogue with someone outside of my comfort zone was the only way to avoid the downward spiral from unhealthy cyclical thoughts. By removing it from your mind and saying it aloud, you are freeing yourself from its tentacles.

Although I was still not sold on the idea of one-on-one therapy, as I felt super uncomfortable talking about any of my ill experiences with anyone other than Dr. Freedman, I did eventually succumb to the idea of group support. I've always loved strangers because strangers were new friends who never had to become old friends; that was my incentive.

I went to group therapy *begrudgingly* and found that it was profoundly helpful and *not* as I envisioned.

It was easy. I didn't feel judged, nor did I feel like I had to appease anyone. I just listened, like I do to my students. I was attentive to other perspectives on illness and experience, which gave me profound insight into my own. And after many weeks of silence, I, too, began to open up as I saw the benefit that sharing my story would have for the others. And with the sound of my own voice in the stale coffee–scented air of the therapy room, I felt like I was snipping away little pieces of myself that were of no use to me anymore. I sent them out to sea to float on without any cares, away from me. I may have even felt a kinship to the group. *Don't tell anyone.*

As a mother, a few years ago, I struggled with the idea of group support once again when I was having a difficult time juggling motherhood, teaching, marriage, and life stuff in general. A coworker and confidante suggested I join a bipolar parent support group. I remember I smiled politely and immediately started to panic, dipping into my endless pocket of silent excuses:

> I'm beyond that. Mothering keeps me grounded. I can't possibly admit I struggle with this, too. And my marriage... Can't I have some secrets? What does all of this have to do with being bipolar? I'm stable now, right?

It was fear that was limiting me once again. I was sinking. I was in my head, not seeking the lifeboat residing in my heart. And as life would have it, a great

H.O.L.D. F.A.S.T.

article from *Psychology Today* magically appeared a day later in my mailbox, with a big red heart on it with the words *keep fucking going* written in beautiful penmanship. The article was entitled "Role of a Support Group in Treatment of Bipolar Disorder" by Russ Federman. The article reads:

> The first posting of this blog (2/1/10) addressed the importance of a support group in the treatment of individuals with bipolar disorder. I'm now returning to the topic, as I think it's an important one that doesn't receive enough attention. I've also found through my years of working with individuals diagnosed with bipolar disorder that the combination of a support group and individual therapy is an ideal combination of treatment modalities. I'd like to explain why.
>
> Most with bipolar disorder experience some degree of stigma due to societal misunderstanding of the disorder. People with bipolar disorder are often perceived as crazy, moody, and unstable. The picture of the disorder conveyed through the media is often one that highlights the more extreme or acute aspects of mood instability. We don't often hear media stories about people with bipolar illness

who are productive and doing relatively well. Beyond these issues of stigma, people with bipolar disorder find that others simply don't understand what they're going through. They might say, "Oh, I understand how you feel" or "I know what you're going through." But the truth is that unless they themselves have bipolar disorder or have had a close connection with someone who does, they often don't know what the bipolar individual is experiencing. Not many do.

The support group environment is one of the few settings where people living with bipolar disorder can truly feel understood and accepted. There's no need to make excuses or to <u>apologize.</u> They don't need to dance around the reality of what's going on. Someone can come to group one night and say... "About a week ago the bottom suddenly dropped out and I've been feeling like crap ever since," and the other group members absolutely know what's being conveyed.

A group member can express that she hates to take her <u>medication</u> and is frustrated with her husband's recurrent response of "It's important for your stability and you should really stick with it." In group, she receives agreement from a member who says, "Yeah, I hate my meds too." Another member chimes in,

"I wish I could stop all my meds and just let my mind do what it wants to do."

The need to hide part of one's <u>identity</u> that's socially unacceptable is absolutely not present in group. In fact, rather than feeling like the outsider who doesn't belong, group members get to feel like they really do belong.

It's the neurotypicals (people without <u>psychiatric</u> diagnoses) that have no place in the group. And the good news here is that the feeling of acceptance and belonging can have a long halflife. It can carry over into the real world and soften the extent to which the individual feels marginalized.

And this is exactly what I did; I joined a support group. I went to a therapist. I talked with Dr. Freedman. I wrote about my endeavors. I started a blog talk radio show entitled *Paging Dr. Freedman: Life Advice to Help You Cope* as another cathartic outlet and way to help listeners. All the things that I was formerly petrified of became part of my lifeboat, the one that keeps me afloat in the everchanging sea.

I overcame my fear by voicing my experiences with mental illness and by opening a dialogue with empathetic strangers.

In summary, in order to explore and understand your illness, you must open a dialogue with someone, or a group of people who can empathize, outside of your inner circle. Their opinions will be more honest, because you are *all* in the same boat. You *can* open up, give your experiences with mental illness a voice, and open a dialogue with those who get it. Chapter 6 will explore your heart space. You will understand that moving into your heart space and out of your cluttered mind will change your perspective and help you integrate new ideas and suggestions into your own methodology and healing.

CHAPTER 6

L IS FOR *LOOK TO YOUR HEART,* NOT YOUR CLUTTERED MIND

Turn off your mind, relax and float downstream...
It is not dying, it is not dying
Lay down all thoughts, surrender to the void...
It is shining, it is shining
That you may see the meaning of within...
It is being, it is being.

—The Beatles

While floating gently like a feather in your lifeboat, contemplating the existence of nothing, *that* is when you are thinking and speaking through your heart space. *That* is when you know that you are *not* your illness. And *that moment* seems very difficult to find when you are trying to juggle bipolar disorder and life. Alas, it is attainable, and it can be yours, even if you are not undergoing deep hypnosis, under the influence of psychedelic drugs, or even levitating. There is no worry of having to be ultrapatient either, as the moment you move into your heart space and out of your cluttered mind, you will just *be*. Patience is strictly a learned thing, and it is taught and utilized in the thinking brain. Your heart is honest.

I always turn to Don Miguel Ruiz, author, seer, teacher, and purveyor of *all* things heartcentered, based on Mexican Toltec Wisdom. His book *The Four Agreements* has been and will continue to be my Linus blanket, as Toltec wisdom has taught me how to turn off my mind, relax, and float downstream, which was undoubtedly The Beatles' way of saying *look to your heart for answers* (in my humble opinion). In other words, Ruiz has taught me to tune out of the confusion frequency in my mind and tune in to the truth and peace that reside in my heart space.

According to Don Miguel Ruiz, the Toltec were spoken of as a nation or a race, but were actually scientists and artists who formed "a society to explore and conserve the spiritual knowledge and practices of the ancient ones. They came together as masters (naguals) and students of Teotihuacan, the ancient city of pyramids outside Mexico City, known as the place where 'Man Becomes God.'"

When I read *The Four Agreements* the first time, I appreciated every word. It satisfied my intellectual curiosity and passion for escapism and folklore. It was truly beautiful. About a year later, after a very harrowing experience connected to bipolar illness, I picked up Ruiz's words again. But that time, I took a deep breath, found a quiet spot, and nestled into the lifeboat in my heart space to read it. There was no judgment there, no comparison, no wandering, no anguish, and no worry. In my lifeboat, I read his words as they are meant to be understood—from a place of love. *Love* is a universal truth.

I learned to quiet my mind by being impeccable with my word. According to Toltec Wisdom, that is the first of the four agreements. Ruiz says to be impeccable with your word, you must do the following:

> Speak with integrity. Say only what you mean. Avoid using the word to speak against yourself or to gossip about others. Use the power of your word in the direction of truth and love.

When I practiced this on a daily basis, it was a form of meditation for me that allowed me to snip away some of the cobwebs and confusion that were running rampant between unjustifiable thoughts. I then learned to trust my intuition by listening closely to and practicing the second agreement:

> Don't take anything personally. Nothing others do is because of you. What others

say and do is a projection of their own reality, their own dream. When you are immune to the opinions and actions of others, you won't be the victim of needless suffering.

It is difficult, as we are inadvertently taught to conform or be judged from a very young age. As an educator now, I feel that gender identity has more freedom, but still has a long way to go. For as long as I can remember, there was a predisposed notion of how I should act as a girl, a daughter, a student, an adolescent female, an adult female teetering on adolescence. I grew up watching my beautiful mother do everything: caretaker, wife, breadwinner, disciplinarian, all while smiling in lipstick, mascara, and high heels. I was to be just like her: pretty, tough, kind, resilient, relentless in pursuits, and still have dinner made, laundry done, and time to laugh with my partner.

For the most part, I succumbed to the "norm" because of peer pressure, acceptance, and fear of bullying by peers. As a teenager, if I veered from what was considered the norm, it was frowned upon, either openly or discreetly. Either way, the negative feelings that were directed toward me actually made me ill; they would manifest themselves as actual illness, both mental and physical. At that juncture in my early life, I did not have the tools to cope. I tuned out completely.

Having read Toltec wisdom, I soon realized that the

negativity I felt as a child, adolescent, and young adult was *their* reality, not mine. With a great deal of the mindful practice of simply ignoring the ill intent of others, I found emotional freedom. When I felt like malice was directed toward me, I practiced thinking from my heart space where there wasn't judgment. I used my heart's intuition; it was in that space where I learned to trust my feelings and let anything that didn't serve me or my family just float away. I now know my truth. You will, too.

My mother used to say, "Amanda, when you assume, you make an ass of u and *me*. Just ask the question." Little did I know when she told me this repeatedly as an indecisive youngster that she was tapping into Toltec Wisdom. The third agreement:

> Don't make assumptions. Find the courage to ask questions and to express what you really want. Communicate with others as clearly as you can to avoid misunderstandings, sadness and drama. With just this one agreement, you can completely transform your life.

With practice, clearly communicating what I want and need has eliminated a great deal of unnecessary discomfort, emotionally and physically. Psychologically, it has provided yet another way to quiet my mind and swan dive into my heart space. It takes the edge off of moments and makes honesty easier to convey and receive. For instance, honesty comes in really handy when I am at home after a long day of teaching and I am overwhelmed. I used to feel like if I succumbed to my exhaustion, I would somehow fail my daughter and husband. I learned that by just being honest, I save myself from overextension, and I clearly state to my daughter and husband that I need a brain break a.k.a. a nap. They totally understand. There was nothing to fear; It was simply me attempting to control everything, when in reality, the only thing I can control is my own action and intention. The fourth agreement:

> Your best is going to change from moment to moment; it will be different when you are healthy as opposed to sick. Under any circumstance, simply do your best, and you will avoid selfjudgment, selfabuse, and regret.

This agreement allows you to hit the off switch in your cluttered brain when all else fails. For instance, in a perfect world, your partner would sense that you are having a bad day or feeling under the weather and would roll out a plush red carpet from your front door to your comfortable bed, tuck you in, feed the pets, and make a beautiful dinner for you and your children. And they all lived happily ever after.

In reality, it is likely that your partner is also having a taxing day, your children are grouchy or antisocial, your pets are shedding, the vacuum hasn't been turned on in

H.O.L.D. F.A.S.T.

two weeks, the laundry is piled high, and dinner *still* has to be made. This is when you can simply do your best. Take a deep breath. There is no anger or resentment necessary; that will only make your bad day or illness worse. There is nothing wrong with a bowl of cereal for dinner. In fact, the kids will probably love it, and the cleanup will be a hell of a lot easier.

When your cranial ship seems to be sinking, know this, and know it in your mind, heart, and soul: *HOLD FAST* and always do your best. It will provide you with a sense of understanding that can only be achieved by accomplishment. I don't care how menial the task; do it with passion. You will find that the little tasks in life, when done consciously and mindfully, become more effective, less taxing, and more meaningful. It is then that you can safely turn off your mind, relax and float downstream— in your lifeboat, of course. This will quiet incessant thoughts of dis*ease*. If we free our thinking from all limitations we have imposed on it, we then realize that the limitless potential of good in the universe is accessible to us.

In summary, experiencing life through your heart space will change everything; it is a place of honesty. You *will* find strength there and see things with clarity. It is being. Just being will allow you to savor life stuff. In your heart, there is no room for *should haves and what ifs*. In your heart space, you will simply enjoy your moments, without the distractions ever present in your mind.

These are precious, fleeting moments. Savor them and drink them in. Engrave them in your heart. Truly, nothing else matters, or ever will. In fact, as difficult as it is to grasp sometimes, it is vastly important that you *know* you already *are* what you want to be. Do your best.

Chapter 7 illustrates that when triggered, looking at the issues with logic will clarify the moment, easing you out of your negative mental state.

CHAPTER 7

D IS FOR *DISCERN TRIGGERS WITH LOGIC* FOR CLARITY

These pains you feel are messengers. Listen to them.

—Rumi

What about when there are very *long* periods between the perfect moments, the moments to be treasured? And what about when you are triggered by something, anything, when it just isn't a good day? It happens. Shit happens. Life happens. And when you're bipolar, sometimes the tiniest match head can be ignited by the most unlikely spark.

Irrational anger is inevitable, but the way you deal with it is what really matters, not the anger itself. This is where logic comes in handy. This is where we have to learn to discern using logic to diffuse a potentially irrational outburst that could cause harm. You can literally reset a negative moment and look at it differently. You have access to your own pause and rewind. There is a *green button*; all you have to do to diffuse the red energy of anger and frustration is push it.

Denise Mann, contributing writer for *BP Magazine*, writes frankly about irritability and outbursts of rage. She highlights very useful strategies to unravel your wrath:

> It starts with a routine annoyance—the living room is a mess again, or another driver cuts you off. Irritation takes hold, then mushrooms as swiftly as a nuclear explosion. Cheeks redden, the pulse quickens, and...boom. Welcome to bipolar rage.

According to Mann, irritable mood is among the primary diagnostic criteria for mania and hypomania. They can also be signs of depression, too.

In my very humble experience, untamed irritability, anger, and rage can have dramatic and devastating effects on relationships with children, family, and friends. In my case, just add alcohol or another mindaltering substance *du jour*—instant insanity. Perhaps more aptly described: instant asshole. It is the truth. I call it, in gentle conversation, a serious case of the

H.O.L.D. F.A.S.T.

crazies, yet it can be intense, painful, and humiliating.

Historically, it has gone a little something like this:

A moment of imbalance rears her ugly head.

The catalyst is generally unknown or vague.

Negative, irrational thoughts begin to flood your mind.

Nonsensical thinking takes over.

The amygdala holds a red flag in front of your third eye.

All defenses disappear.

Blood boils.

Weird, erratic emotions take precedence.

Inexplicable, odd, and most times, obscene things spew from your lips, hopefully not coupled with aggressive movement (that happens, too).

- o Something weird happens.
- o There is a moment of silence or downward glances.
- o Your moment of confusion passes.
- o A bucket of hypothetical cold water is thrown over your head.
- o The red flag is removed from the third eye.
- o All three eyes see a look of complete disgust and fear on recipients of outburst.

- Immediate shame sets in.
- Guilt and regret take over; they are ruthless.

Does this sound painfully familiar? Denise Mann writes the following:

> It's easy to detect changes when a normally easygoing person starts to get cranky. For people whose temperaments are marked by "hostile personality traits" — impatience, frustration, rudeness (such as interrupting when others are speaking) — there may be a more subtle crescendo.

Like the personalities of every person with the affliction, triggers are all different, and there is no magic pill to cure triggers like a dose of *Trigger Be Gone or Insanity Stop*. Well, they exist in some capacity, but the debilitating side effects are not worth the chemical numbness, in my humble experience.

So this is where discernment and logic come into play. They are the holistic approach to mental wellness and a much healthier approach to avoid impending irrational emotional upheaval. Time and space become important; the logical mind needs to know they exist when you feel like you're going to blow.

In your lifeboat, there is a tool kit available to you. In it, you will find an audio track, cradled by your favorite sound.

H.O.L.D. F.A.S.T.

Simply push the *green button* that *says diffuse*, listen closely, and let it go.

1. When you push your *green button*, you will be cradled by the sound that you *need* and a voice you *want* to hear. The voice will gently, deliberately, and slowly instruct you, kindly:
2. Slowly exit the situation. For example, if you are driving, find a safe place to pull over and do the breathing exercises.
3. If you are in a room full of people who are about to feel your wrath, remove yourself.
4. Find a quiet place, or at least a place where you can be alone with your thoughts.
5. Picture your favorite color or a color that calms you.
6. Fill your mind with that color.
7. Picture it like swirls of soft light, softening every nook of your mind and body.
8. Deeply breathe in the color through your nose to the count of four.
9. Hold the breath and color for four seconds.
10. Feel the softness of the color pushing into every part of you.
11. Make a mental note of the good feeling. Remember it. Hug it.
12. Exhale out of your mouth to the count of four; every exhale sends the negative feelings and energy away, like smog.
13. Just breathe.

14. Do this continually until you feel the subtle calming in your mind.
15. Picture the bad feelings and smog drifting into nothingness and harming nothing.
16. 1This will diffuse the moment, if not change your mood drastically for the better.

Allow logic to remind you that if you still feel offkilter, remove yourself from the situation, completely, and *know* what calms you when you are finally alone. For me, it is taking a brisk walk and focusing on my breath:

1. I breathe four long seconds in through the nose, four long seconds out through the mouth for the entire duration of the walk. It works wonders.
2. If the situation allows (or even if it doesn't), I take off my shoes! Terra firma is imperative. Bare feet change everything. Connecting, literally and figuratively, with Mother Earth calms and will soothe and center you, too.
3. Picture your favorite color again as a beam of light coming down from the universe, entering your crown chakra at the top of your head, permeating your body with warmth, going down your spine and legs, through the bottom of your feet, and through the earth, all its beautiful levels, to the core.
4. Tie a loose bow at the core of Earth with your ribbon of colored light.

H.O.L.D. F.A.S.T.

5. Tie another loose bow and up, up in the universe with your ribbon of colored light.
6. Immerse yourself in the strength and stability; feel like a tree feeding from the earth. You will not fall.
7. Feel the energy permeate you.
8. Take deep breaths, then untie your ribbons and start walking.

The stability will stay with you, I promise. The more you practice this exercise, the more in tune you will feel with your own emotions. And the more in tune you feel with your emotional self, the easier it will be to clear the cobwebs in your mind and dive into your tranquil heart space. You can lounge in your lifeboat, swim freely in the sea, and avoid irrational outbursts. The only thing there is, is love. That is a universal truth.

The clarity of mind you will feel by exercising these diffusion tactics will allow you to reassess the situations that trigger you so that you can stop, rewind, and start fresh—before the damage is done. Just picture the *green button* and push it.

In summary, Hippocrates nailed it when he said, "The physician treats, but nature heals." We need to be conscious of our triggers to deal with them in a healthy way. Nature helps. Take deep breaths, walking and moving away from the situation. We innately know how to heal ourselves if we just listen to our bodies; our bodies will tell us what we need to diffuse the moment before it explodes. Practice mindfulness; pay attention to what derails you.

Chapter 8 will illustrate how internalizing any anguish is counterproductive. It manifests itself in unpleasant ways, like lashing out family or friends. The best way to cope is to take a deep breath and dive into whatever is causing the anxious feelings, even if you can't see the bottom.

CHAPTER 8

F IS FOR *FACE ANXIETY* AND DIVE IN

> You better stop, look around
> Here it comes, here it comes,
> here it comes, here it comes
> Here comes your nineteenth
> nervous breakdown.
>
> —The Rolling Stones

And that is exactly how you should say it! Shout It from the rooftop! "Here comes my (whatever number) nervous breakdown, and I haven't any idea why I am anxious in the first place!" Voicing it and owning it will take away its power; it cannot debilitate you if you don't allow it. You have a choice.

For someone who suffers from anxiety, an anxiety

disorder, or anxiety exacerbated by bipolar illness, specifically mixed states, can oftentimes feel impossible to overcome in the moment; it is real to you, and that gives it power.

Alas, in your lifeboat, there are some pretty clever ways to get to the other side of anxiety without falling to pieces. There are very specific tools available to you that reside in your heart space, right when you need them.

To truly understand tools to overcome anxiety, it is vastly important to look at it as a list of symptoms that differ for everyone. According to the *National Institute of Mental Health*, some symptoms of anxiety can include and are not limited to the following:

- Feeling restless, wound up, or on edge
- Hyperactivity
- Trouble sleeping
- Fatigue
- Difficulty concentrating
- Irritability
- Muscle tension
- Difficulty controlling feelings of worry

The beauty of this list is not the symptoms, but the fact that when you experience one or several of them, and that feeling of impending doom begins to sink into the *whatif* territory in your solar plexus, you *are* in control! This is where you have the opportunity to put the kibosh on the prospective panic attack. Why? Because you already own it! Why? Because you *know* what is happening and will choose to sit with each symptom and hold its hand like a child.

That is what anxiety symptoms are like: tantrums in toddlers. All they need is to be acknowledged and loved. That changes everything. So hold your own hand and tell yourself what feeling is creeping up. Then say it out loud—shout it, if need be! Seriously!

According to anxietycoach.com, an invaluable resource for those seeking to overcome anxiety disorders, it is actually your reaction to shame and embarrassment that produces unwanted symptoms:

> Shame and embarrassment and uncomfortable feelings which fuel the idea that you have something to hide, some aspects of yourself which are so negative that you figure you should prevent others from noticing them. This leads to secrecy, a powerful force behind social phobia.

It's funny how anxiety manifests itself in different ways, yet there is one universal truth: keeping anxious feelings secret, or keeping the symptoms camouflaged behind false emotions, will only make the situation worse. The urge to keep your flaws secret leads you to oppose the symptoms. As anxietycoach.com states:

> The path out of Social Anxiety Disorder is

so much easier when you come to see that secrecy is not your friend; that others will generally be accepting of your flaws as you are of theirs; and that is when you give up your efforts to hide and oppose your visible anxiety symptoms, that's when they become less frequent and disturbing.

HOLD FAST to the knowledge that anxiety is inevitable and to fight it is counterproductive. Instead of swimming against the current of your own emotions, swim with them. Instead of fearing the unknown beneath the surface of the water, tell yourself, "I am excited" instead of "I am anxious." Say it out loud. It *will* incite a completely different feeling and help you skate right over the slippery moment. Practice this.

Swim to your lifeboat in your heart space. Remember to *revisit* discernment. Open your tool kit. Gently push the green button that says diffuse. Listen closely and let it go. You will be cradled by the sound and voice that you *need*. It will deliberately and slowly instruct you down from your ledge. You must face it to float through it, no matter how big the wave of anxiety. And one day, you will surf it, forgetting that it was ever frightening to you.

Remember, when you push your *green button*, slowly exit the situation. For example, if you are driving, find a safe place to pull over and do the breathing

H.O.L.D. F.A.S.T.

exercises. If you are in a room full of people who are about to feel your wrath, remove yourself. Find a quiet place, or at least a place where you can be alone with your thoughts:

1. Picture your favorite color or a color that calms you.
2. Fill your mind with that color. Picture it like swirls of soft light, softening every nook of your mind and body.
3. Deeply breath in the color through your nose to the count of four.
4. Hold the breath and color for four seconds.
5. Feel the softness of the color pushing into every part of you.
6. Make a mental note of the good feeling. Remember it. Hug it.
7. Exhale out of your mouth to the count of four; every exhale sends the negative feelings and energy away, like smog.
8. Just breathe.

Do this continually until you feel the subtle calming in your mind. Picture the bad feelings and smog drifting into nothingness and harming nothing. This *will* diffuse the moment, if not change your mood drastically for the better. *HOLD FAST.* This, too, shall pass. Just ride it out.In summary, stop dipping your foot in the water. Gently splashing yourself will not make your entrance easier. You have to face the unknown *headon*.

Just dive in. Remember, it is *excitement* you are feeling for the unknown, not *anxiousness*. This knowledge *alone* will change everything. Chapter 9 will illustrate that fear is inevitable in any unknown situation. Expect it, embrace it, experience it, and let it go.

CHAPTER 9

A IS FOR *ANTICIPATE FEAR*—EXPECT, EMBRACE, AND EXPERIENCE IT

> We are all on the same trip;
> different rivers, same ocean.
>
> —Me to myself, August 8, 2012

It is so important to remember this as a person when we start to defeat ourselves. It is a humbling approach to looking at life, another universal truth; we are all in this together, no matter what river we choose to explore. We all end up in the same ocean, and that ocean will wash away the bumps and bruises from our journey.

Once, when I was particularly down when my daughter was a toddler, I asked Universe for some advice. I was in a dark place, pretending to be light for my little girl and falling to pieces during the fleeting moments when she napped. Historically, when I found myself drowning in that place, I hid. The fear was so difficult to overcome that I could not see beyond the task in front of me. So I asked Universe, Goddess, God, whoever or whatever energy suits you in a time of prayer, contemplation, and need, and she answered.

I closed my eyes, poised a pen, and I wrote what I heard in my mind's eye. I questioned nothing. I didn't care if it seemed nonsensical or sounded like a drunken journal entry from high school. What I wrote felt right. And when something feels right, that is when you can assure that it is from your lifeboat, floating gently in your heart space. Universe told me,

> It is the fear that is the big mystery, Amanda. What are you afraid of? What is the worstcase scenario? We are all on the same trip; different rivers, same ocean. Just float. Fear is an illusion. It is a defense mechanism to keep you from moving forward into a better way of life.

I read and reread what I wrote and my unjustifiable fears subsided. I went to check on my daughter, who was napping in the soft late afternoon light of August, and lay down on my bed to enjoy the peace. As I drifted off, I reached over to adjust the sheer curtain on my window and brushed my hand against a pile of books stacked on top of a wine crate next to my bed. A book that I hadn't visited in many moons fell to the floor: *30 Day Mental Diet by Willis* Kinnear. I picked it up to place it back on the pile and missed; the book lay open to a page with a coffee stain on it. In bold letters it read,

STOP BEING AFRAID: Don't Defeat Yourself.

I blinked several times, and as much as I wanted to just go to sleep, I couldn't ignore it; it beckoned to me. Kinnear wrote,

> For the most part people seem to go through life being afraid of one thing or another. In fact, many appear to go out of their way to find things to be apprehensive about. Their thoughts emphasize what they are fearful of and overlook those things in which they may have complete confidence and security. In spite of all appearances and situations, of one thing you may be sure, and that is that there is nothing like the nature of Life Itself that holds anything against you.

I rubbed my eyes and sighed. I asked, and Universe answered, loud and clear. Kinnear continued,

> When you fear, you have completely forgotten the childlike trust you used to

have in your world. Instead of maintaining a calm assurance that things will be alright, you apparently have developed a perverse nature which looks out on the world with a jaundiced eye and the only things you see or anticipate are not good. This attitude of course takes all the joy and happiness out of living. Even when you should be enjoying life you find yourself immersed in a maelstrom of fear about what might happen.

Fear is nothing but the reflection of your own negative attitudes. So I poised my pen again and said, "Thank you, Universe. Please tell me more." And I wrote,

> The only thing to avoid...is avoidance. Avoidance only prevents you from moving forward. Avoidance is another manifestation of fear, and one that makes overcoming even more difficult with time. Avoid avoidance Amanda; you will develop a healthy sense of personal control by simply smiling at fear and inviting her in for coffee. Listen to her, she has a purpose but it is fleeting. Be deliberate with fear, like conversation with an acquaintance. Accept her as a guest, enjoy the conversation, collect the coffee cups, thank her for stopping by,

> and politely show her the door. You have life to attend to, and no room for extra guests. She will leave, and she will knock at your door from time to time. But you will be deliberate and tell her the truth, not avoid her because only truth resides in love. You will open the door, look into her eyes and you will speak to her from your heart space; tell her that there is no room for her in your lifeboat, send her on her way and shut the door. Your family needs you.

I closed my journal, thanked the Universe for stepping in, and heard my little girl babbling in the next room, waking from her slumber. All the while, somewhere in my mind, I heard the crackling of a radio playing FDR saying his 1933 inaugural address. I question nothing:

> So, first of all, let me assert my firm belief that the only thing we have to fear is fear itself—nameless, unreasoning, unjustified terror which paralyzes needed efforts to convert retreat into advance.

When I had accepted fear by embracing it and experiencing it, I was able to respond more rationally, and move forward. When I was able to see the situation for what it was, I became mindful of what made me uncomfortable. Anticipation works the same way for *any* situation. Never, ever question whether or not your situation warrants as much fear as you are feeling. Accept it! Whether it is skydiving or simply walking into a family gathering, surfing a twelvefoot wave, or picking up a potentially unnerving telephone call, fear is *fear*. It is real to you.

When you have accepted it, you are able to question it and perhaps reframe it in your own mind. When you are in the moment of acknowledgment of fear, having already anticipated it, ask yourself the following questions:

1. Why do I feel this way?
2. What about this situation makes me uneasy?
3. Can I pinpoint exactly what it is that is making me feel uncomfortable?
4. Can I give this feeling a voice?
5. Can I give this feeling a face?
6. What is the fear under my fear?

Write it down. Examine it. Embrace it. Experience it. This will allow you to reframe the language of your fear by making it a powerful statement, rather than a *whatif* moment.

In life, I have had to face *many* fears that I was able to *avoid* for many years, prior to becoming a parent. By accepting and questioning each fear, I have been able to overcome things that I thought weren't possible for me; my daughter is the reason. There simply is no room in the

H.O.L.D. F.A.S.T.

life of a parent to succumb to selfcentered fear when a child is involved.

There was a time in my life when I was paralyzed by prospective family gatherings. I could not handle the energy. I always felt like I was being judged and made myself physically ill with fear of interaction. My only way to cope, I thought, was to drown myself in alcohol, in addition to whatever other substances, legal or not so legal, were floating around in my brain. I used to drink myself into a state of temporary selfacceptance, then exited stage left as soon as I felt the subtlety of discomfort creep back up my spine. Inevitably, with each exit or failed attempt at showing up for a gathering, the guilt I felt about not being present for family, mixed with the fear of ill judgment from family, made each fear exponentially worse. It was a vicious cycle.

With parenthood, I was forced to get over myself. It took the emphasis off of me and put it on the importance of my daughter's experience. The thought of skipping out on a social event, simply for a self centered fear that makes me *ill*, is inexcusable. I vowed to myself that she *will* experience everything that will make her life as rich as it can be, and I *will* simply have to reframe my fears to benefit her. For example, "What if they look down their noses at me for this, that, and the other thing" has become "My daughter will know her family, make friends, and form relationships that matter."

In summary, embracing fear can be a less harrowing journey. With practice and reframing of ideas, it will become something that you can safely anticipate, embrace, and experience to grow. You *will* overcome. Chapter 10 illustrates that in order to get through your emotionally debilitating periods, you *have* to step up to the challenge and own it. Read on.

CHAPTER 10

S IS FOR *STEP UP* TO YOUR FAMILY CHALLENGES

> Let everything happen to you
> Beauty and terror
> Just keep going
> No feeling is final
>
> —Rainer Maria Rilke

When you are so down and truly wish you were a ghost or that you could wear an invisibility cloak simply to avoid any human interaction, family or not—these moments that are actually the most important. These moments of complete despair give you one opportunity that only comes with hitting the shitbottom of the abyss, emotionally. Rung by rung, even on *fragile knees*, you can only go up, or drown in the muck and the mire. And when

I say fragile knees, that is a very gentle way of saying that one more ounce of emotional weight could very well take you to a cold, stagnant quarry and drop you in the water, attached to anchors. It is these very, very difficult moments when the mere prospect of even speaking to another human or emerging from your cocoon sends you into a tailspin so dizzying, you don't think you'll ever see straight again. This is where you must step up; there truly isn't a choice in the matter.

Mrs. D's success was a difficult process at first, as beginnings can be. But as she went through the motions, and with each rung of each step, it became a little bit more clear and a bit easier for her to move forward:

- *H* is for *honest*
- *O* is for *open a dialogue*
- *L* is for *look to your heart*
- *D* is for *discern with logic*
- *F* is for *face anxiety*
- *A* is for *anticipate fear*
- *S* is for *step up*
- *T* is for *trust the process*

Mrs. D stepped up to her illness, allowing her to experience her emotions again. She is in control, and not her disease. I can proudly say that she now surfs the wave of life and parenthood as the best she can and shares her story with those who falter. She is *truly* an inspiration, and I know she will share her learned methodology with those who need it, too.

H.O.L.D. F.A.S.T.

The truth is, you can and you *will*, too. With every rung up the ladder of emotional difficulty, out of the muck and the mire, each step up will become less daunting with continued pursuit. Acknowledge and accept each step up for what it is; don't try to change it. See each step out as your truth, letting go of feelings of inadequacy, guilt, shame, jealousy, fear, and loathing. Just snip them away like weeds; let them fall back down to earth to feed her.

When you reach each new step, you must forgive yourself and others attached to each one prior to move forward. The past is irrelevant. Move forward. You must let them go and forgive; guilt and shame have no place in selftrust. You cannot step up without trusting yourself, and you cannot be there for yourself, family, or friends if you don't step up to the challenges. By disappearing completely, you are practicing avoidance. And as discussed, the only thing to *avoid is avoidance* because that is just another manifestation of fear. Mrs. D had to completely recreate her fears into positive affirmations:

Instead of "My daughter wants to go away to boarding school because she hates me and I am a terrible mother," she gave it a new spin:

> Despite my distance, I have done the best I can, and my daughter is a testament to that. I will support her in any academic decision that she makes. She is both intelligent and independent. I will be here

for her, regardless.

Mrs. D stepped up to the challenge of parenthood, stared her fears in the eye, and regained her power. She took a fearbased emotion and changed it into excitement.

According to psychcentral.com, an excellent online resource about bipolar disorder and its many manifestations, showing your family and friends that you can do it will give you the confidence you need to pursue the next thing. "Bipolar disorder is hard on relationships," says Sheri Van Dijk, renowned psychotherapist and author of *The DBT Skills Workbook for Bipolar Disorder*.

She continues by saying that "the very symptoms—swinging moods, risky behaviors—often leave loved ones feeling confused, exhausted and like they're walking on eggshells."

She also sees that loved ones have difficulty distinguishing between the illness and the person. They might invalidate the person's feelings and either blame everything on the illness or believe the person is making conscious choices when it is the illness:

> "Bipolar disorder is difficult to understand," Van Dijk said. "Different affective episodes, [such as] depression versus hypomania, result in different symptoms, and one episode of depression or hypomania can be different from the

H.O.L.D. F.A.S.T.

next within the same person."

So it's incredibly important for loved ones and friends to get educated about the illness and how it functions. Individual therapy, family therapy, and support groups can help. Refer loved ones to selfhelp resources and biographies of people who have written about their experiences or memoirs of people with bipolar disorder.

According to Van Dijk, "Getting a handle on your emotions also improves relationships." Whether it is with your immediate family, your acquaintances, workmates, or most importantly children, working on assertiveness is key. Individuals with bipolar disorder tend to have a tough time being assertive. As we know, to *step up* and climb out of a dark place to be there in truth, you have to work at it, stepbystep, rungbyrung; you must *HOLD FAST*, and therapy is a great place to learn assertiveness skills.

Van Dijk suggests using "I statements": "I feel _____ when you _____." She gives the following example:

I feel scared and hurt when you threaten to leave me.

For instance, I *know* how changeable my personality can be, and when under stress, I tend to flounder between two extremes, rapidly, despite having more control than I used to. I can feel my mood fluctuate from moment to moment, and I know that even though I try to keep it quiet, my daughter, husband, friends can inevitably feel it.

One day when I was particularly "off" and compulsively cleaning to avoid interaction, my daughter asked me.

"Mom, are you okay? You seem a bit...off." She was seven. I took a deep breath, dropped my mop, and pulled her in for a gigantic hug.

"I'm okay, River... Sometimes I just get a little overwhelmed." I smiled. "But it is certainly nothing that you have done to make me feel this way."

"What do you mean 'overwhelmed'?" she asked endearingly.

I thought about it for a minute.

"Well, you know when your head is so full of great ideas that you just don't know which one to focus on? Like 'should I read a book, color, draw, play with my dolls, or go outside on the trampoline?' And all the while, you *know* that you have to complete a mathematics practice worksheet for your class on Monday, too, which you don't feel like doing?"

"Yes! That's the worst." She rolled her eyes. "I mean, honestly, who would want to do homework when you could play outside, instead?"

"I know, right?" I laughed.

H.O.L.D. F.A.S.T.

She knew the feeling, intimately, in her own little kid way.

She and I spent the next hour playing a *game*. I decided to cool my jets and do what was important. I was never taught to be assertive and, by nature, am very nonconfrontational. It was a real struggle for me in life to overcome this and assert myself in necessary situations, so I implemented Van Dijk's "I statements": "I feel ____ when you _____" into our game. It was like Mad Libs, sort of.

"River, fill in the blanks. I feel _____ when you _____."

She immediately chimed in, "I feel sad when you are sad."

I felt like crying, but instead said, "Good, good! Now try another."

"Hmmm. How about 'I feel happy when you play outside with me'? Now *you* try one, Mom."

"Okay." I took a deep breath. "I feel full of love when you smile," I said.

River gave me a huge hug and giggled.

"I've got one," she said. "I feel full of gas when you make chili."

We laughed uproariously, and my mood shifted considerably. Children know how to do that without even trying.

Since that discussion, I ask her to fill in the blanks every now and again. The best part? Even if she is silly with me, I have noticed her asking very direct questions to other kids and her teachers, and being much more transparent with her feelings. And that is a gift! She is not afraid to voice her emotions.

Just last week, she seemed a bit down. When I asked gently if she had a difficult day at school, she shrugged. That is generally a telltale sign that something is amiss in third grade.

"Katie wasn't her happy self, Mom, and she was acting weird toward me. It made me very upset."

Katie is one of her best buddies in school, and I knew there had to have been more to the story.

"Did you and Katie get into an argument?" There was silence, then uncontrollable sobbing. "I don't know, Mama. It was just very strange.

We couldn't agree on *anything* today, and my heart hurts."

It was the end of the school day, and I knew that Katie was still in the school building. "Well, how about you go and talk to Katie and tell her how you feel?" Begrudgingly, we walked hand in hand into the school to find her. I watched, proudly, as River ran up to her friend and said, "Katie! I'm so sorry we disagreed a lot today."

H.O.L.D. F.A.S.T.

They gave each other a big hug, and that was the end of that. Children are amazing. Conflict. Resolution. Done. No avoidance. No questions asked.

Simply voicing the emotion is the first step up. I am so grateful that this thinking has been instilled into her; communication truly is the key.

The fear of confrontation and the inevitable anxiety that figuratively chokes a bipolar person such as myself is an ongoing challenge. When trying to complete seemingly menial tasks, Van Dijk stresses the importance of using relaxation techniques and not using avoidance behaviors. Instead of avoiding the situation, model the behavior of children who think from their heart space, unless they are taught not to. Revisit the following steps from chapter 7, where you move from your brain approximately eighteen inches down to your heart space and settle in right there:

1. I breathe four long seconds in through the nose, four long seconds out through the mouth for the entire duration of the walk. It works wonders.
2. If the situation allows (or even if it doesn't), I take off my shoes! Terra firma is imperative. Bare feet change everything. Connecting, literally and figuratively, with Mother Earth calms and will soothe and center you, too.
3. Picture your favorite color again as a beam of light coming down from the universe, entering

your crown chakra at the top of your head, permeating your body with warmth, going down your spine and legs, through the bottom of your feet, and through the earth, all its beautiful levels, to the core.
4. Tie a loose bow at the core of Earth with your ribbon of colored light.
5. Tie another loose bow and up, up in the universe with your ribbon of colored light.
6. Immerse yourself in the strength and stability; feel like a tree feeding from the earth. You will not fall.
7. Feel the energy permeate you.
8. Take deep breaths, then untie your ribbons and start walking.

As Van Dijk explains:

> The more you avoid things because of your anxiety, the more your anxiety will actually increase, because you never allow your brain to learn that there's nothing to be anxious about.

The calm that you find will give you the strength to step up to whatever or whomever it is that you would rather avoid. The more you practice this, the easier it will become. Scaffold this new way of thinking with psychotherapy. It is tremendously helpful for managing bipolar disorder and the above challenges. Please, as tempting as it is to forego psychiatrist appointments,

H.O.L.D. F.A.S.T.

because it *just is, just go*—and tell the truth. Transparency is key. You *will* step up. You *are* needed.

Another very important thing to note: If you've been prescribed medication, never stop taking it abruptly—this boosts the risk for relapse.

In summary, to *avoid* avoidance behaviors and step up to the challenges of life, you must practice. Move your thinking and decisionmaking from your headspace to your heart space; *that* is where truth resides, and that is where your strength to step up will come from. Utilize psychotherapy, take your medicine habitually, and practice, practice, practice.

Read on.

Chapter 11 will show you that you have to trust yourself and the process. It is not selfish to fasten the literal or figurative oxygen mask on yourself first, then on to your loved ones. It is in preparation to be selfless and present for your family.

CHAPTER 11

T IS FOR *TRUST THE PROCESS—* TRUST YOURSELF

> It is clear that we must trust what is difficult;
> everything alive trusts in it, everything in Nature
> grows and defends itself anyway it can and is
> spontaneously itself, tries to be itself at all costs
> and against all opposition. We know little, but
> that we must trust in what is difficult is a certainty
> that will never abandon us; it is good to be
> solitary, for solitude is difficult; that something is
> difficult must be one more reason for us to do it.
>
> —Rainer Maria Rilke

You are exactly where you need to be right now, in this moment. It is your place, your purpose, and your lesson. What happened yesterday, an hour ago, five years

H.O.L.D. F.A.S.T.

ago has dissipated into the ethers; that was then. Be in the *now*. If you take a moment and mentally drift through memories of how you got here, you will see that every second that has passed—every memory, tragedy, comedy, love, misery, person, and fleeting emotion has brought you right here. Trust it. Trust yourself. You are in control and can only be there for yourself, family, and friends if you are present. What is being present? It is being conscious in the moment, and it requires asking yourself different questions:

- ✓ Is my mind where my body is right now?
- ✓ What can I feel in my body right now?
- ✓ What is perfect about this situation right now?
- ✓ What sensations can I feel in my body right now?
- ✓ What is my breathing like right now? Is it shallow and fast? Slow and deep? Nose or mouth?
- ✓ What is the temperature of the air?
- ✓ What do I like to do when I am not thinking about the past/future but just enjoying what I am doing? Painting? Running? Yoga? Writing? Cooking? Baking? Drawing? Playing?
- ✓ Whatever it is, do more of it.

When we are *not* present, things can go awry. Perhaps you've experienced one or all the following signs that you are figuratively out to *lunch*:

1. You forget how you got where you are.
2. Your thoughts race day and night.
3. You avoid situations where something could go wrong.
4. You can't remember the last thing you ate.
5. Nothing seems fun anymore.
6. You think everything is a steppingstone to the future.
7. You are bad with names.
8. You and your phone are inseparable.
9. You feel disconnected from people.

    I spent the majority of my younger life *out to lunch*, for one reason or another. But like everything else for me, that dramatically changed with parenthood. For example, I never understood why on a plane, the airline attendant directions asked you to fasten an oxygen mask to yourself in the event of an emergency before attaching it to a child or loved one. It always seemed so strange, so selfish—until I flew for the first time with my daughter. Frank, me, and our little River boarded an *Alitalia* international flight to Croatia when she was just eight months old. We were going to visit my dear friend Sanja in Croatia to introduce her to her new little friend. And as many budget international flights go, there were many connections, and it was an especially long journey.

    In the wee hours of the morning, an hour or so before landing in Liverpool for our first connection, I rocked little River in my lap, fighting off sleep, gazing

H.O.L.D. F.A.S.T.

around the twilight cabin at the sleeping faces, mouths agape, window shades halfmast. Blearyeyed, I listened to Frank softly snore beside me as I read the overhead panel above our row:

> Attention: in the event of loss of cabin pressure, oxygen masks will come out of the overhead compartment. Please fasten a mask to yourself, before fastening a mask to your child or row mate.

And in the twilight, staring down at my sleeping baby, I finally understood why I would attach the mask to myself before River or Frank; to help anyone else, you have to help yourself first. It is another universal truth. Give your feelings a moment to just breathe, then act. It is then, in any situation, that you are balanced enough to trust your own judgment and do the right thing. It is truly a selfless act. I was present.

Rilke said, "Each experience has its own velocity according to which it wants to be lived if it is to be new, profound and fruitful. To have wisdom means to discover this velocity in each individual case."

Inevitably, things will change if you are willing to trust the moment and look at them differently. And to trust is a pure emotion. Trust comes from love and love lives in your heart space. Floating in your lifeboat, there are no wrong emotions, only different kinds of emotions. Judgment does not work in the heart space.

When it comes to your family and friends, you must trust your decisions. When you trust your mind, your family and friends will trust your direction and choices. *You* will trust your direction. In that place of love and trust that reside in your heart, there is selflessness. That is your true self, and the self that will be there for your family.

As Rumi states, "Don't you know yet? It is *your* light that lights the world."

What you trust and imagine puts that very thing, that very reality into motion. If you trust and imagine harmony, it is harmony you will experience. It truly is as simple as that. Trust only exists in love, and thinking through love only comes from the heart space. Trust your intuition, and, as Dory said in *Finding Nemo*, "Just keep swimming."

As a parent, the most important part of my personal journey was to learn to listen selflessly to my daughter, without jumping on the "you're wrong and I am right, just because" bandwagon. The verdict is still out with my partnerincrime (and he would most certainly agree), but with our daughter, listening was a skill I had to train my cluttered bipolar brain to let go of, and let my heart space do the thinking. Listening requires being present, and when you are present, you are living in truth. Truth resides in the heart space, and you have to practice moving your thoughts from your brain to your heart. Practice the seven steps to become present:

H.O.L.D. F.A.S.T.

- ✓ Is my mind where my body is right now?
- ✓ What can I feel in my body right now?
- ✓ What is perfect about this situation right now?
- ✓ What sensations can I feel in my body right now?
- ✓ What is my breathing like right now? Is it shallow and fast? Slow and deep? Nose or mouth?
- ✓ What is the temperature of the air?
- ✓ What do I like to do when I am not thinking about the past/future but just enjoying what I am doing?
- ✓ Whatever it is, do more of IT.

In time, you will catch yourself zoning out and will be able to reign yourself back into the moment. It is in your heart space, in truth and love that you can truly listen to others without judgment. Try it.

There is a wonderful article by Jane Nelsen that I found in my journey, compliments of family education.com, a reputable and a many times inspirational reference point. In the article, the contributors recommend the following to become better listeners:

Children will listen to you, after they feel listened to. Listening—it's not as easy as it sounds. It's often uncomfortable to really *hear* somebody else's point of view (especially if it's your child and she's right and you happen to be wrong). You might hear something you don't want to hear. It's uncomfortable to be challenged. You might hear something that challenges your belief system or makes you question your assumptions about life. You might hear something that will make you want to *change*.

Here are some excellent reasons to work on your listening skills:

- The main difference between *taking* and *talking* is one little letter, l. That l stands for listening. To talk with somebody, you've got to listen.
- Listening carefully is how you gather information about what's going on in the other person's head.
- Listening effectively builds strong relationships.
- Listening thoughtfully shows respect.
- Listening is always the first step in solving problems.
- Listening to other perspectives will teach you a lot.
- Kids are smarter than most grownups think, and they generally know what they need.
- Listen to your kids, and they will teach you how to raise them. Listen to others, and they will teach you how to treat them.
- If you want someone to listen to you, you'll need to first listen to her.
- A person who is listened to learns how to listen. And until she learns how to listen to you, it's the same as telling your problems to

the bathroom mirror—no matter how eloquently you express yourself.

With others, listen first and listen from your heart space before reacting. The true story may take a while to emerge; the real feelings may take time. If you need to, count to ten and trust. With children, as familyeducation.com states,

> Kids aren't always organized, and kids with emotions (and last time I checked that was all of them) are even less so. It's hard for a child to wait until an opportune time to raise an important issue or disclose some vital information about how she got sent to the principal's office or that Toby beat him up because he accidentally shoved him into the garbage can. Sometimes a child will fret over telling you something important— and let it slip out just at the moment you are least expecting it. Perhaps you're on your way out the door to a board meeting, or making a lefthand turn into the most dangerous intersection in town, or checking that the soufflé hasn't fallen. Trust me, when you're least prepared is when the most vital information will slip from your child's little lips like a sigh. Carpe diem—seize the day! Keep a

constant lowlevel awareness, a sense of priorities. If Bobby is in hysterics or Sally is desperate to tell you about her date, perhaps you can rearrange your morning (and your life) and listen. (Can you call in sick? Cancel the carpet cleaner? Get somebody else to pick up for the carpool? It's important!).

In summary, in order to trust yourself, you must trust the process. In order to trust anything, you must approach it with clarity. It is essential that we are present when dealing with our friends and loved ones. If we react to them from a place of nonlove, the outcome can be detrimental. We can trust our heart space, because only truth and love reside there. To be present, move out of your mind and into your heart space to do your thinking and listening. By doing this, you are being honest with yourself and your loved ones. Trust yourself and trust this process, and you will teach others, through your action, to do the same.

In chapter 12, you will inevitably ask yourself, "What if?" and understand the obstacles that you may face in starting a new way of thinking. You will understand the paradox of speculation—your desire to find certainty creates more uncertainty and worry. Congratulations! You now have all of the tools to radically change your life. Read on.

CHAPTER 12

WHAT IF THE WHAT IFS NEVER HAPPEN?

You have to keep breaking your heart until it opens.

—Rumi

What if it doesn't work? What if I fall apart? What if my partner is not supportive of my endeavors? What if my children are not receptive to me? What if I fail, and even scarier, what if I succeed and everything falls into place for me? What if I no longer feel defined by my mental illness? Who will I be then, and what will be my excuse for erratic behavior? What will my friends think of me then?

Your lifeboat is full of tools. When speculation rears her curious little head into your progress, and says, "Okay, but what if..." and your desire for certainty begins to create more uncertainty and worry, just stop. Breathe. Slide out of your brain, into your heart space again, and into your lifeboat. Remember, it is chockfull of invaluable tools to keep you afloat in life, above the stormy water and downward spiral. Let's review:

- H is for *honest*
- O is for *open a dialogue*
- L is for *look to your heart*
- D is for *discern with logic*
- F is for *face anxiety*
- A is for *anticipate fear*
- S is for *step up*
- T is for *trust the process*

Lifeboat compartment #1: honesty buoy. By inflating your honesty buoy, you will show your family and children what is truly going on inside of your mind and open a line of trust that may not have been there prior to this.

Lifeboat compartment #2: logic galore, as logic will help you rise to the surface when inundated with selfdoubt. It is in moments of whatif when the logic buoy comes in handy to get you back on course; HOLD FAST to the sail and intuitively steer downwind. Feel the *whatif,* then snip it away like a stray thread, and send it into the universe. Eventually, it will lose its power and fall away, sinking into the abyss in the bipolar sea. In lifeboat compartment #3, you will find the fear and anxiety anchors that are directly attached to the whatifs. However uncomfortable it is, you must experience the negative emotions, the unknown, embrace it like a loved

H.O.L.D. F.A.S.T.

one, even as it scratches, bites, and tries to pull you under where you cannot breathe. You have to feel its weight, listen to it, give it love, rock it gently, then allow it to silently fall to sleep in your arms. Remember, it is only then that you can let it go gently and watch it sink in hindsight.

As Lead Belly sings, "Sail on, sail on, little girl, sail on... Go on, sail on, little girl, sail on/You gon' keep on sailin'..."

Yeah, but what if the whatifs *do* happen? I distinctly remember sitting in a doctor's office for a followup examination after I was diagnosed with a tumor on the pineal gland in my brain. I happened upon an article in *Psychology Today*, "Fighting Life's 'What Ifs'" by Edward H. Hallowell. Hallowell stated the following:

> Worry is like blood pressure: you need a certain level to live, but too much can kill you. At its worst, worry is insidious, invisible, a relentless scavenger, roaming the corners of your mind, feeding on anything it finds. It sets upon you unwanted and unbidden, feasting on the infinite array of negative possibilities in life, diminishing your enjoyment of friends, family, achievements, and physical being—all because you live in fear of what might go wrong. People who worry too much suffer. For all their hard

work, for all their humor and willingness to laugh at themselves, for all their selfawareness, worriers just cannot achieve peace of mind.

Worry is amazingly common. At least one in four of us—about 65 million Americans—will meet the criteria for an anxiety disorder at some point in our lifetime. Even those individuals whose lives are going well may worry excessively on occasion. And yet, worry is a very treatable condition. Most people today are not aware of all that we have learned about worry in the last 50 years. Just as rainstorms may strike in different ways—sudden thunderstorms, lingering drizzle, occasional showers—so does worry attack its victims variously. We've come to understand the many distinctly different types of worry, and the underlying triggers. Worry may accompany simple shyness, depression, generalized anxiety disorder, or even posttraumatic stress disorder. Each kind of worry responds to specific and powerful techniques, from cognitive therapy to medication to regular exercise.

Hallowell later states that "Worry

sometimes begins with a negative possibility, a mere 'What if?' Then it burgeons up out of information that originally was neutral or innocuous. One of my patients, Becky, calls these endless 'What ifs?' SBPOWs, which stands for 'spontaneously branching polymers of worry.' (She pronounces SBPOWs as 'spouse' because she claims her husband is the source of most of them.) 'A little worry can branch spontaneously with a vengeance,' she explains. 'It's like a pattern of frost that shoots across a cold pane of glass. In seconds I am fighting with an enormous net of dangerous, intricate detail. You can't believe how quickly I go from dealing with one worry to having a jumbled mess of them.' This kind of worrier broods incessantly. When the mind obsesses over negative outcomes at the mere hint of one, the worrier is suffering from a type of obsessivecompulsive disorder (OCD). About 5 million Americans are afflicted with OCD, and though we do not have a cure, we do have excellent treatments that can drastically reduce the severity of the symptoms. In OCD, worry rules the mind like a sorcerer. The individual even resorts to superstitious rituals in the hope that the rituals will magically rid him of the dangers he senses and fears. I once treated a man who had to hop on one foot whenever he was waiting in line, because he felt he would be in extreme danger otherwise. The sufferer of OCD is obsessed with a variety of intrusive, unwanted thoughts. He also feels compelled to act out certain rituals in an attempt to stave off (imagined) dire consequences associated with his unwanted thoughts."

I was interrupted by an agitated nurse who had been trying to get my attention while I was immersed in the article. "Miss Grieme!"

My mother snapped. "Amanda!"

"Oh, I'm sorry." I fumbled with the magazine. The nurse impatiently waved me on toward the neurologist' office, as I tore the article out and folded it into my pocket. The nurse glared at me. My mother rolled her eyes at my very deliberate thievery.

"Oh, I'm sorry. I should've asked. I didn't mean to deface the magazine."

She sneered. "Yeah, that was an accidental tear, fold, and fall into your pocket, I presume, too."

H.O.L.D. F.A.S.T.

She rolled her eyes at me and showed me to the examination room. It worked. I felt like a jerk.

I had been suffering a series of debilitating headaches and vision impairment spells that I thought were completely random. After a good month of consistently weird episodes while working at a restaurant, I decided to tell my parents. They made an appointment with our family doctor for an exam and an MRI.

Of course, I didn't consider that the strange headaches and vision impairment had anything to do with taking antipsychotics and SSRIs and washing them down with copious amounts of Bombay Sapphire Gin and Guinness. Nor did I consider my diet of cigarettes, marijuana, coffee, occasional meals at 3:00 a.m., and almost daily smatterings of any narcotic available could've had any bearing on my condition. What did it matter? I was highfunctioning, a good employee, a grad student on a fullride assistantship, and just straight up...well... invincible.

Alas, the very brief-but-humbling discussion with the neurologist changed my tune. He sauntered into the room and smiled. "Amanda, this is a small tumor on the pineal gland in your brain."

He put the images up on the screen to exhibit it. "This is what we call an accidental finding, and think it hasn't any correlation to your symptoms. In fact, it may have been there since birth, we don't know. But we will watch it month by month for a year to see if it grows, because to operate on it would be deeply invasive and not worth the risk involved if it doesn't have to be addressed."

I sighed with relief.

"Although we did study your labs and found that your blood tests don't show any signs of malignancy, but they do show many other signs that could be leading to your debilitating headaches, fainting spells, and vision impairment."

He had my attention.

"Amanda, not only are your minerals very deficient and vitamin D extremely low, your blood pressure is also low. We were compelled to perform a blood drug screen test on your whole blood specimen to check levels for your prescribed psychiatric medications."

I honestly hadn't even considered recreational drugs.

"We used immunoassay screening with reflex for definitive testing."

I knew where the conversation was headed and just wanted to get up and leave middiscussion.

"We found trace amounts of narcotics and opiates that are not prescribed for you and a hot urine test, a.k.a.

marijuana in your urine." The neurologist looked at me. "Amanda, you understand that mixing prescribed psychomeds with street meds can cause serious brain damage and heart damage, if not accidental death, yes?"

"Yes, I am aware of that." I nodded.

"Okay, and you do realize that *all* of your symptoms could be a direct correlation to drug use and abuse in general?"

"Yes, I am aware of that, too." I nodded. "Well, I see this as a blessing in disguise!" He clapped his hands together. "Here is a referral to a dual diagnosis psychiatrist that specializes in bipolar disorder and addiction. Dr. Ladaudio is a much better fit for you, and he is right down the hall on your left."

Before I could say anything, he said, "He has your MRI brain images, your medical history, and your blood test results and urinalysis. My nurse will see you out. We will follow up in a month to check on the status of the brain tumor, but all signs point to a benign incidental finding."

He smiled and shook my hand. The nurse escorted my mother and me down the hallway to Suite 200, Constantine Ladaudio, MD.

My mother looked at me. "So?" "So, what?" I hissed.

"Psychiatrist specializing in dual diagnosis, Amanda? What's that all about?"

I shrugged. "Not really sure."

My mother sighed and gave me a sideways glare. "My ass you're not sure." She was relieved that the tumor was seemingly benign and grateful that the doctor called me out on my poor lifestyle choices.

Twentythree years later, the article "Fighting Life's 'What Ifs'" by Edward H. Hallowell still sits on my bookshelf. I look at it from time to time to remind myself of a major reality check that I had early on. It is still very pertinent today, a universal truth.

Something else to note: Please remember, speculation turns one fact into infinite facts. Acknowledge her (speculation) inquisitiveness, embrace her curiosity, then send her overboard with a flotation device. There is not enough room for her in the lifeboat in your heart space.

In summary, examine the whatifs and acknowledge them, but move beyond. Focusing on the worry aspect of anything is counterproductive. The bottom line is this: What if I don't try? That is when the whatifs truly matter. You must experience the discomfort and move through the challenge.

Chapter 13 will show you by working with me and integrating the *HOLD FAST* method into your life, you will be able to start anew; you will be able to reign in

H.O.L.D. F.A.S.T.

bipolar symptoms and be present for yourself, loved ones, and coworkers. A once seemingly bleak and difficult situation will become easy to maneuver. A successful, nurturing, and gratifying life with bipolar disorder is your new reality, the beginning.

CHAPTER 13

HOLD FAST—IT IS YOUR BEGINNING

> Hold fast to dreams, for if dreams die, life
> is a brokenwinged bird that cannot fly.
>
> —Langston Hughes

By integrating the *HOLD FAST* method into your life, you can start anew. You will be able to reign in bipolar symptoms and be present for yourself, family, and friends. A once seemingly bleak and difficult situation will become easy to maneuver; a successful, nurturing and gratifying life with bipolar disorder is your new reality. Welcome to the beginning: your *me* can now get over your *myself*.

Let's meditate on this for a moment, you and me:

You are resting in your lifeboat, nestled gently into

H.O.L.D. F.A.S.T.

the calm sea in your heart. You're enjoying the warmth of the sun, the tranquility of the water, the gentle rocking, when you hear, "Mom...Mom."

At first, it is just a distant hum, a crescendo, a bird flying somewhere in the distance.

"Mom...Mom."

The bird has come closer. You see it soaring in front of the sun, casting a moving shadow across your lifeboat. Your gentle rocking becomes a bit more apparent. Perhaps there's a wake from a passing boat? Wait, you are the only lifeboat here, so...

"Mommama."

The bird is now closer; you laugh at the soft scene.

The bird is calling in ¾ time—a Tchaikovsky waltz.

How lovely!

"Mom! Wake up! I can't find my [fill in the blank]! It is urgent!"

Your eyes snap open; your child is three inches away from your sleeping face. Take a deep breath.

"Finally! You were snoring so loud! I need your help finding something!"

This is where you exhale. Smile, sigh deeply, rub your eyes, and *know* that your lifeboat will be there when you need to climb back in. Instead of nestling back into your cocoon, you can help your child or whomever needs you find whatever it is that she needs to find. However small it seems to you, it means the world to her. That second of connection alone will change her perspective and strengthen your relationship. This is it:

- *H* is for *honest*
- *O* is for *open a dialogue*
- *L* is for *look to your heart*
- *D* is for *discern with logic*
- *F* is for *face anxiety*
- *A* is for *anticipate fear*
- *S* is for *step up*
- *T* is for *trust the process*

You, without even trying, have just opened up your line of communication with your loved one by being present and showing the value of the moment to her. You overcame your urge to hide and made yourself available and willing to help.

You are well equipped to sail on, to surf the wave, to *HOLD FAST* to today. You are present and aware and understand:

- o Honesty and transparency are essential to healing.
- o Seeking support and opening a dialogue outside of your immediate circle *will* shine new light on your situation.

H.O.L.D. F.A.S.T.

- Moving out of your mind and into your heart *will* change your perspective.
- Examining your triggers logically *will* ease you out of a negative mental state.
- Fear and anxiety are inevitable. Embrace them, experience them, and let them go.
- Owning your illness *will* get you through the darkness and back to what matters.
- Self trust and selfcare are not selfish and are essential to being present for yourself and your family.
- Abolish guilt. When you examine it from afar, it just doesn't have the same bitter taste. The cold, lonely shudder that you inherently feel in your solar plexus *will* not overcome you.
- Guilt is very different from a distance, and from your lifeboat in your heart space, it is just a passing cloud.
- Remember, in life, guilt has an entirely different wardrobe, but the same silhouette in shadow. The feeling is there when things are amiss, and there is no justification for it.
- Where there is unconditional love, there is the propensity for more guilt. It is yet another confusing facet of our human condition.

I close with words and philosophy that I covet from psychologist Dr. Doris Jeanette. The *Philadelphia Inquirer* proclaimed Doris Jeanette "The Siren of Spontaneity," noting that "her cotherapist is Nature." Dr.

Jeanette states:

Guilt is the worst experience known to humans. Guilt ties you up in knots and makes you feel unworthy and miserable. Guilt is not a real emotion. Webster defines it as "the fact or state of having committed an offense, or wrong against moral or penal law." Guilt is caused by thinking you have done something wrong. You think you have done something wrong because you judge yourself or someone else judges you. A child does not "feel guilty" until someone tells her that she has offended someone or hurt someone's so called "feelings." It is a conditioned response, not an authentic emotion. In other words, you are taught to feel guilt when someone judges you—about anything—how you dress, how you move, how you think, what you do. Guilt is a form of manipulation.

Dr. Jeanette has taught me to become conscious of my judgment of myself; once you cease making yourself wrong, it becomes easier to deal with other people's judgment of you. For instance, letting go of others' opinions of you is imperative. It doesn't matter what he or she thinks. What matters is that you are acting from a place of truth and love. She taught me that attending to my own needs and honoring them, rather than making them wrong, is okay.

Her insight emphasizes awareness, noting that being aware that judging someone else as wrong is the same thing as judging yourself as wrong. Let it go, forgive

H.O.L.D. F.A.S.T.

because forgiveness is really nothing more than giving up your own judgment. As Rumi said, "You are not a drop in the ocean. You are the entire ocean in a drop."

HOLD FAST, friend! You *will* ride this out.

ABOUT THE AUTHOR

Diagnosed at the age of twenty with rapidcycling bipolar disorder with schizoaffective episodic delusions, it was not until a decade after A. Grieme's own mental tumble that she was not so gently shown her path to be a mental health awareness advocate. Today, she lives to share how she stayed afloat in this evercycling existence and to help others understand they can, too.

It was while she was curled into herself, cradled uncomfortably into the corner of her parents' couch following a psychotic episode, that she found her way out of her own hell with a pen and paper. It was all she could do, the first step in the separation from an insidious diagnosis that did not allow itself to be ignored. Despite the ever present fog and deleterious effects from prescribed little blue and pink pills, she deemed *imagination slayers*, she wrote letters.

H.O.L.D. F.A.S.T.

The letters documented her fall to those she loved and admired, here and gone. As A. Grieme says, "With each letter, a piece of MYSELF, smothered by rapid cycling bipolar disorder slowly unraveled, detangling the knot that choked the essence of who I am: ME."

A. Grieme resides with her family outside of a tiny town in Northeastern Pennsylvania. She is an author and teacher and chooses writing, coaching, teaching, and radio as her creative, cathartic mediums to help others. Her life experience with mental illness, self medication, and almost two decades in education lends her readers, students, clients, and listeners invaluable, empowering, often quirky life advice, braided in a message of hope.

Grieme is also the author of H.O.L.D. F.A.S.T.: Ride out Parenting with Bipolar Disorder (2020); Paging Dr. Freedman (2019); Dear Prudence (2009), the inspiration for Paging Dr. Freedman); and Motherhood Made ME Get Over MYSELF (a published blog, 2014), and an interactive workbook entitled Loving Yourself and Others with Mental Illness (2022).

Contact A. Grieme

Email: agriemebooks@agriemebooks.com

Radio: www.spreaker.com/show/holdfastradio

Website: www.agriemebooks.com

THANK YOU

Thank you, kindly, for reading this book. I *know* that you are on the path to understanding. Bipolar disorder can really pose a challenge for those of us juggling the many facets of life. As you've learned, it can be done! It is a delicate balance but one that can be achieved. *HOLD FAST!* You, *too*, will ride out this storm..

To share my gratitude, I'd like to invite you to contact me with any questions; I am here to help. Please feel free to email me at agriemebooks@agriemebooks.com. My mission is to help those who doubt themselves through this evercycling existence and to share in hope, laughter, and the sheer lunacy of it all. Thank you *again* for including *me* on your *journey*.

Fondly,

On fragile

knees,

A. Grieme

Printed by Libri Plureos GmbH in Hamburg, Germany